# SHE'S CRAZY, HE'S A LIAR

## Now What?

## CECILY KNOBLER

Published by Robert Kennedy Publishing
400 Matheson Blvd. West
Mississauga, ON
L5R 3M1 Canada
Visit us at **RKPubs.com**
         **ShesCrazyHesALiar.com**

**Managing Senior Production Editor:** Wendy Morley
**Art Director:** Gabriella Caruso Marques
**Acting Art Director:** Jessica Pensabene
**Editorial Designer:** Ellie Jeon
**Illustrator:** Cal Slayton
**Illustrator Conceptions:** Wendy Morley
**Proofreader:** James De Medeiros
**Back Cover Photo Credit:** Jeff Nicholson, The Shot Photography

Library and Archives Canada Cataloguing in Publication


Knobler, Cecily, 1971-
     She's crazy, he's a liar, now what? : the single girl's guide to understanding
the sexes / Cecily Knobler.


ISBN 978-1-55210-069-1


     1. Man-woman relationships.  2. Single women.  3. Dating (Social customs).
I. Title.


HQ801.K65 2010            646.7'7082            C2009-906921-0


10 9 8 7 6 5 4 3 2 1

Distributed in Canada by
NBN (National Book Network)
67 Mowat Avenue, Suite 241
Toronto, ON
M6K 3E3

Distributed in USA by
NBN (National Book Network)
15200 NBN Way
Blue Ridge Summit, PA
17214

Printed in Canada

Dedicated to all the
ones who got away...

# •Table of Contents•

# INTRODUCTION

In a bookstore recently I was amazed at how many books there were on the subject of how to "get a man" or "pick up women." The guidebooks ranged in titles, from simple catchphrases to clever, dirty ones. I was both intrigued and horrified that there seemed to be such a big consumer need for lessons on pursuing love and sex. While I stood for a mere five minutes in the "self-help: relationship" aisle, at least ten women and six or seven men appeared, sifting through these books like they were the long, lost Dead Sea scrolls. Amazing!

Well I've been through it all more times than the average bear, and I'm not kidding. I've dated from the west coast to the east coast. I've traveled through the United States, Europe and the Middle East, just to meet, fall in love with, and get dumped by nearly every guy out there. (That might be a *slight* exaggeration … but only slight.) So with that kind of experience I must be able to offer something new with regard to meeting, dating, sleeping together and ultimately navigating the break-up between a man and a woman.

Through it all (so far, anyway) I've decided these countless experiences might actually help me in my pursuit of self-actualization. And so I would like to share my findings with you. However, I urge you to take it all with a grain of salt. I am, after all, a really weird, perpetually single stand-up comic.

> "Thirty seconds after you're born you have a past and sixty seconds after that, you begin to lie to yourself about it."
>
> – David Cronenberg

I'll never forget the first time a guy called me psycho. I'd been playing four square with a group of fellow fourth-graders and suddenly had the urge to throw the big red ball into a nearby garden so I'd have my hands free to grope J.J. Nesbitt. I wrapped my tiny, ten-year-old arms around his waist, puckered up and kissed him on the cheek. He screamed a ridiculously high-pitched squeal, ran behind the teacher and declared me a crazy person. Actually, the exact term he used for me was "psycho-mamma," which was odd, considering he wasn't a 40-year-old disco dancer, circa 1976.

For the life of me I couldn't understand why this would be his reaction. I was no supermodel, but for a fourth-grader I wasn't bad. How could he resist my long dark hair and awkward pre-teen teeth? More importantly, how could he be so *cruel*?

Turns out that last one was a question I'd be asking for the next 20 years. How … *could* … he … be … so … *cruel*? Of course the names of the boys changed throughout the years, as did the nature of our relationships, but the sentiment remained the same. Guys had no heart, it seemed, and we women had too much of it.

Being older now (and a little bit wiser), I'm more able to empathize with that other gender. I know now that most of the thoughts and feelings I assigned to boys in school never existed. So, for example, if a guy looked at me in the hallway with his eyes half-squinted, he probably wasn't angry with me; he was stoned. What he was really and truly feeling I couldn't know, and so I made it up. Now, thanks to social networking sites like MySpace and Facebook, I get to hear from guys I've dated along the way and find out the truth. For better or for worse, I get to see myself through their eyes and memories. And let me tell ya, sometimes it ain't pretty.

I remember one guy – let's call him Patrick. He emailed me 13 years after high school to tell me he was surprised I ended up in the entertainment world, as I'd been so shy. He said he had always thought I was cute, but didn't ask me out because I never expressed opinions about *anything* and seemed to be interested in nothing but designer clothes and gossiping. I was furious when I read this, as anyone who knew me even remotely at that time knew I had opinions about *everything* and was far from shy.

But what he got really wrong were my interests. The only thing I ever remember caring about in high school (besides getting into an Ivy League university) was *Patrick*. How could he have missed that? How could I have failed so miserably in communicating to him that he was the one for me, and that my whole existence revolved around him feeling the same way? Though other girls my age were (allegedly) sleeping with some of our teachers, I had my eyes set on an age-appropriate senior. And while I had thought I was wowing him with my long stares and hair-flips, he was seeing me as vapid and *gasp* uninteresting!

How could we have seen things so differently? Of course, now I've come to realize that most men and women approach love and sex and talking and just about *everything* from a completely different perspective. The question now is: *why* does each gender think the other is certifiably insane?

# CHAPTER 1

# he said • she said

A lot of the words I hear tossed about by my female friends when discussing guys include: liar, asshole, withholder, biaaatch. (That last term is relatively new, but holds true nonetheless.) There are, of course, variations on these terms. For example, "liar" sometimes becomes "lying sack of s#$%" or "biggest lying asshole in the world" or "couldn't tell the truth to save his own ass from a fire." You get the idea.

When it comes to describing women, many of my male friends use terms like: clingy, crazy, psycho, emotional wreck, nut-job, whack-job, freak-job, (guys love anything with the word "job" attached, don't they?) Again, there are different versions of these terms, and sometimes guys like to just use them all at once: e.g. "She's a clingy, crazy, psycho nut-job."

Sure the name-calling gets reversed sometimes (i.e., she's a liar, he's insane), but nine times out of ten (at least in my experience) it's *he* doesn't tell the truth; *he* runs away from true love; *he* withholds his emotions and *she* calls too much; *she* needs too much; *she's* a psycho.

Let's take a look at some stories from both sides and see if we might make sense of it all. (Of course, names have been changed to protect the not-so-innocent.)

## DAVID AND PENELOPE

Penelope literally spotted David from across the room at a crowded party, as cheesy as that might sound. She actually used the word "strapping" when describing him to a friend: "Check out that guy with the dark hair, the one in the green shirt. He's hot and I think he's been looking at me."

And he had been. David, being very shy, had been trying to steal glances of Penelope all night. For one he thought she was cute, but more importantly he liked that she'd been eyeing him, especially since he felt he was terrible at meeting women. After some back-and-forth eye-molestation, Penelope finally made a move over to the veggies and dip area, where David had been lingering all night.

"Excuse me," she said, reaching across him to grab a carrot.

"Oh no problem," he flirted. "Can I help you dip that?"

From there, the door was open and both David and Penelope walked right on through. They exchanged phone numbers and the next day David called to set up a date, which Penelope happily accepted (despite not loving his phone voice). It was set; they would begin their courtship that Friday night.

Now let's freeze this story for a second. Up until this point, both Penelope and David would agree on the facts. They did meet at a party and hit it off. What happened after that, when told by either David or Penelope, is quite a different tale.

## PENELOPE'S VERSION

David, who was oddly 15 minutes early for the date, buzzed my apartment from the lobby as I was trying to get my mascara applied. I told him I'd be right down, but secretly cursed him for being so early. When I got downstairs, he was looking straight up at something on my ceiling.

"Hey there," I said, putting my hand out to give him a half-hug.

"Hi," he answered enthusiastically. "I was just noticing your building's crown molding. It's so beautiful!"

I hadn't ever really noticed.

"It's amazing." He was sweating at this point.

I remember those details well, because they struck me as so odd. Why was he sweating? And why did he seem so genuinely impressed with my run-down, slum apartment building?

He drove us to a trendy Moroccan restaurant, which I'd mentioned on our previous phone call. Before we'd even sat down, I suddenly became extremely anxious. The hostess said it would be a 20-minute wait, and I immediately headed for the bar. David suggested that instead we "take a stroll around the neighborhood" and I wanted to vomit.

"Nah," I'd told him. "I think we should get some wine."

He agreed. In fact, there was little so far that he hadn't agreed with, which for some reason was making my stomach turn. We ordered our drinks. Once I'd had a few sips I felt better, and started to wonder why I was being so hard

on this guy. He was adorable to look at and was sweet and had a lovely job as a political researcher. He even smelled good. But there was something about the way he hung on every word of mine that just seemed unsettling.

The hostess came back over and said something about being sorry, but somehow she'd forgotten to write our name down. David gave her a warm smile and said, "No worries." I wanted to say, "Ya know what, David? WORRIES!" but I didn't. Instead I excused myself to the bathroom to call my mother, who told me to relax and perhaps take a Valium or "something in that family." I'd told her I shouldn't have to take a muscle relaxant to get through a date, but she respectfully disagreed.

When I got back to the bar, David was chatting away with the bartender about environmental issues. I scanned his neck and arms for any sign of a tattoo … any sign of an *edge*. He had none that I could see. He did, however, ask me if I'd put on new lipstick. I hadn't, so even that question bothered me. What was wrong with me?

Once we were finally seated (and I'd had two glasses of wine) I felt a little better. That is, until he relayed a story about how he'd read the self-help book *The Secret*, which he believed was the catalyst for all of his dreams coming true. I downed my third glass of wine and jokingly asked, "Am I one of those dreams?"

As earnest as one could be, he looked me straight in the eye and said: "Yes. I put a picture of a beautiful woman on my vision board and here you are."

"You're joking, right?"

"Do I look like I'm joking?" he'd said.

I felt like this was way too much to bear, but the alcohol in my liver didn't agree, so we ended up making out later that night. I was just getting over my annoyance with him when he confessed he was a virgin. I found this funny and yet intriguing, so I ended up dating him for three months. I tried to de-flower him the whole time but it got too frustrating, so I called the whole thing off.

## DAVID'S VERSION

From the second I picked Penelope up, she seemed like a bundle of nerves, but I've always liked that in a woman. It took her forever to come downstairs and she seemed distracted when I tried to discuss the architecture of her building. But she looked awesome and I was jazzed to start the date.

When we got to the (overpriced) restaurant, all she wanted to do was drink. This seemed kinda weird to me but also totally sexy, so we sat at the bar and I let her do her thing. She seemed happier once she got her booze. Just as we were starting to ease into things, the hostess came over to say our wait would be longer than expected. I thought Penelope was gonna rip her head off, but luckily she just drank some wine.

She got flirtier over dinner and occasionally would even put her hand on my knee or shoulder. I noticed that her drinking intensified, but the more she guzzled, the more into me she seemed. Plus I was driving, so it was all cool.

I was pleasantly surprised when she invited me up to her place at the end of the night. I had an awesome time kissing her, although I found it was kind of weird that she stopped halfway through to do a shot of Baileys. She then proceeded to try and remove my pants. I thought maybe that would be a good time to reveal my big secret to her, so I sat her back down on the couch and

took her hands. She made drunken eye contact for a second and then kind of just stared off into Merlot-space.

I told her, "So, you might think this is sort of weird, but there's something you should know."

She yanked her hands away and started rambling stuff like, "You're married? You're gay? You're a woman?"

"No, none of that stuff. Actually, I'm a virgin."

I expected her to be surprised. What I did *not* expect was for her to laugh for the next six minutes straight. "But … but … you're 30!"

"Yeah, well, I've been waiting for the right one."

She laughed a little longer and then started kissing me, so I figured the news was okay by her.

I really liked this girl. She was odd and patronizing and anxiety-ridden, but at the same time, she was funny and smart and sexy. We ended up dating for just over three months and just when I'd decided she was the one I wanted to lose my virginity to, she dumped me in *my* car, claiming her feelings just weren't there. I was heartbroken and kind of pissed off that I'd wasted so much time on someone who wasn't feeling it.

## WHERE DID IT GO SO WRONG?

Perception and self-delusion are to blame. Penelope wasn't being honest with David or even herself about how he made her feel. It's pretty clear to us outsiders that the majority of the time she wasn't enjoying his company. Perhaps she thought it would be good to try going out with a different type of guy, but it was unfair to continue this charade at David's expense. It also seems pretty obvious that Penelope didn't respect David and was insensitive to his vulnerabilities. She shouldn't have laughed at his virginity and no, whatever her mother might say, she shouldn't have to take prescription meds to get through their courtship.

For David's part, he seems to have taken on the masochist role quite willingly. He's a smart guy; he should have been able to tell that Penelope was too

wound up for him. (Case in point: having someone laugh in your face right after you've shared something intensely personal isn't a good omen.) David chose to ignore the signs and, just as she thought she could make him edgier, he thought he could save her. Never works, believe me.

Bottom line: both David and Penelope were hoping the other would ultimately become somebody else. This just doesn't happen and it's a good thing they figured it out relatively early.

Note to you guys out there: If you're a "David" type and consider yourself a nice guy, don't be discouraged if not all women go for it. I can confirm that many women have their own issues they need to work through and you shouldn't stop being a good guy just because we can sometimes be nuts. This book's title does begin with "She's Crazy," after all. Remember, in the '80s movie *Say Anything*, Lloyd Dobler remained a good man and he got the girl in the end. So yeah, sometimes it really isn't *you* … it's *us*.

And for the "Penelopes," stop trying to change good guys into bad boys. They will eventually resent you, as will the poor women who have to date them after you've broken their spirits. If you *must* date a naughty boy (and I'm not saying you *should*), find one who's already broken, won't you?

## ANDREW AND SARAH

These two potential lovebirds met on Match.com. Andrew had described himself as "smart, loyal and *ready*." He'd posted a snappy picture of himself wearing a pinstriped suit and another of him literally running on the beach with a child on his shoulders. (If he'd really been going for the jugular, he should have posted a photo of himself bottle-feeding a Labrador puppy.) He'd said he was looking for a woman who "gets it" and who had "read classic literature," and he'd listed himself as having a

slender build at the age of 39. (FYI, he declared he wanted to find a woman between the ages of 22 and 30.)

Sarah had been delighted to read this post. While at 34 she was out of Andrew's requested age range, she felt confident that her sense of humor and Princeton education would more than make up for being four years too old. She also had supplied the site with lovely photos, even though Andrew would later admit he wasn't sure of her body type.

Sarah sent Andrew a "wink" (or a nudge or a lick or whatever it is that dating site allowed) and a quick message to say hi and introduce herself.

*"Hey there 'Big Andy 200'*

*Noticed your profile and thought you seemed intriguing. At the very least, you don't seem like a serial killer. Also, you're cute!*
*Check out my profile and let me know if you want to maybe meet for coffee?*

*Signed, Princeton Princess 75, (real name Sarah)"*

Sarah was unsure if she should include the "you're cute" part, but figured somewhat desperate times called for desperate compliments and plus, he really *was* cute. It turns out it was the right move at the time, as Andrew responded well to ego boosting. He took a look at Sarah's profile and wrote back the following:

*"Dear Sarah,*

*Very nice to meet you. I should tell you right up front that I am a serial killer, but I only go after blondes and since you're brunette, we should be okay. How's next Tuesday for you at Starbucks on Sunset and LaBrea?*
*Let me know if this works.*

*Best, Andy"*

 ANDREW'S VERSION

When I got to Starbucks, Sarah was already there sipping on some kind of Frappuccino with whipped cream. Her face looked like her picture, but she had described herself as athletic, and really she was pretty underweight. She seemed jittery and nervous. When I approached her, she stood up and spilled her drink. I caught it before it hit the floor and said, "You must be Sarah. I'm Andy." She laughed a very loud, almost grunty laugh and said, "Nice to meet you."

The coffee date went pretty well. We had a lot in common and although I wasn't sure if there was a strong attraction on my part, I was interested enough to stay and chat for two hours. As we were leaving we had an awkward hug and just as I was about to say, "I'll send you an e-mail," she said, "Wanna go have a drink this weekend?"

I was ambivalent, so I said, "Sure, why not?" We exchanged phone numbers, I called her and we made a date for cocktails that Saturday of the same week. She definitely seemed into it.

Flash forward to Saturday, when I picked her up and took her to my favorite watering hole in Hollywood. (I'd made it pretty clear on the phone that this was just drinks and I figured since I was picking her up at 9:30, that she'd have eaten.) When we walked into the bar which also happened to be a Mexican restaurant, she said "I'm totally starving." There went my plans to sit at the bar.

After she was nice and tipsy from her double-shot margaritas (and full from her nachos and taco platter) she did offer to get the bill. When I said, "No, I got it," she replied "thanks" and quickly put her wallet away, proclaiming she'd get it next time. She barely had time to get that last sentence out, as shortly after, her tongue was in my mouth. That's where it remained for the next four hours.

It was a fun night and she was a great kisser, but overall I just felt the chemistry was off. I didn't want to take it to the next level as I felt that would be leading her on, so I did the right thing and didn't call her for another date.

## SARAH'S VERSION

Andy was late getting to Starbucks and the second he arrived he knocked over my mocha frap. Luckily he caught it before it spilled, but I was immediately annoyed. He was cute though, *very* cute, and we proceeded to have an outstanding conversation for the next couple of hours.

In fact we clicked so well, I broke one of my standard dating rules. I asked him out to dinner that weekend. He was all for it and later in the week he called and said something like: "he'd take care of the planning."

I guess what that meant to him was picking the cheapest, darkest dive he could find, but I figured I'd make the best of it. He was still super cute and the chemistry was absolutely there. We chowed down on chips and tacos and delicious margaritas and I was so sure this was the perfect date I even offered to pick up the tab. He, being a perfect gentleman, refused. It was just getting better and better and it hit a peak when Andy finally leaned in to kiss me. We made out for the rest of the night. He tasted amazing and he was such a great kisser, I even considered inviting him back to my place. I didn't, figuring I could wait at least one more date before devouring him.

At the end of the night he told me he'd call soon and I knew for certain that he would. I literally swooned for days after that and somehow didn't notice that two weeks had gone by and I hadn't heard from him. 'He must have lost my information,' I thought. 'That was the best date I've had in years.' I finally sent him an email through Match.com boldly asking when we were going out again. After an entire month, I finally received an email back that said, "Had a great time with you. Been really busy and think I want to try to work things out with my ex-girlfriend."

## WHERE DID IT GO SO WRONG?

I guess it would be easy for me to immediately call Andrew a tool, but that won't teach us much, so let me attempt some objectivity and say there really is no right or wrong in this situation, only differing perspectives. Oh please. Who am I kidding? They both f#&%ed up and we can actually learn something from their mistakes.

In this situation Andrew failed to disclose his true feelings. Probably hoping he might change or discover them, he had every right to accept a date, but once he knew the chemistry was lacking, he really shouldn't have made out with Sarah all night. That said, he is only human with sexual urges and we do need to give him credit for not taking it further than it went.

Here's where I stop being nice with regard to Andrew. He should have called or at least sent an email to explain to Sarah that his feelings at that juncture were not mutual. Also, there was no reason to mention an ex-girlfriend. Even if it were true (and not the lame, made-up excuse it was), the mention of her would only serve to hurt or confuse Sarah more than she already may have been. Tool. (Sorry, I couldn't resist.)

Sarah screwed up because she jumped the gun. Yes, they had a lovely conversation and yes she found him very attractive, but that is not a contractual obligation. It just so happens that sometimes feelings of lust or love, or even like, go unrequited. Even though Andrew, insensitively, did kiss her for hours (and yes, one might see that as a sign of interest) he had a right to change his mind.

Maybe Sarah could have waited before opening herself up emotionally. I'm all for kissing when you want to kiss and calling when you want to call. I truly don't believe that there are rules that apply to everyone at all times. But we all (both men and women) have to be aware of our personal guidelines. If we kiss someone on the first date (for hours) and they never call, will we be crushed? If so, we might want to hold off on the physical and emotional intimacy until we have more information.

## CALEB AND DIANE

These two were set up on a blind date after being shown each other's MySpace photos. Their mutual friend Dave had worked with Caleb at an accounting office and knew Diane through his sister. Based on very little, Dave decided they'd make a great couple, and since neither was getting a whole lot of dating action on their own, they agreed to go out.

After a couple of cutesy emails, they decided to meet at a hip bar on the Upper East Side of Manhattan. Diane had wanted to keep the date relatively close to her apartment, just in case he turned out to be a dolt. Caleb, who lived in the East Village, was pretty laid back and didn't really care where they met, just as long as he got out of his apartment for a while.

Caleb arrived first and was already sitting at the bar when Diane got there. They were both relieved when they saw each other, as both were more attractive in person than they appeared in their photos. (When does *that* happen?)

Diane threw her purse on the bar and cozied on up next to Caleb. They gave each other a quick hug and Caleb asked Diane what she wanted to drink. So far, based on just first impressions, this date was going very well.

 DIANE'S VERSION

I was absolutely overjoyed to see how cute Caleb was and thought it was chivalrous of him to immediately ask me what I'd be having. Since I'm not too into alcohol, I ordered a Sprite and told him I might get wacky and order a White Russian or something later on. He seemed to think this was cute.

After his third Jack and Coke, we'd talked about pretty much everything under the sun: his trips to Paris, my love of whale watching, his siblings, my affinity for tea. It was an easy conversation with few lulls and growing intrigue. Finally, when he ordered his fourth drink, I went ahead and "got crazy" and asked for a small Amaretto Sour.

We continued to have a pleasant conversation, which reached a climax when we started making fun of our mutual friend Dave. I laughed so hard sweet and sour juice came out of my nose. And then the bill came.

What happened next sounds fabricated, but I can assure you it's not. The bartender put the bill directly between us, and Caleb promptly put his hand in

his pocket and pulled out a calculator. He said the following: "So I believe the guy should pay exactly 55 percent of the bill and the woman, 45 percent. Does that sound fair?"

It didn't, especially seeing as how I only drank a fraction of what he had (and subsequently owed only a fraction). But it wasn't *that* that bothered me, really. It was the fact that he had a calculator in his pants on our *date*! How could he have even *fit* that in there without my noticing? (And for the record, this was not a calculator on his PDA or cell phone. This was a large, old-school calculating machine!)

I quietly nodded and waited for him to calculate my 45 percent. I then finished my drink, said, "Great to meet you. Keep in touch," and headed for home.

 CALEB'S VERSION

I got to the bar on time but Diane was at least 25 minutes late, which I thought was a little thoughtless, especially since she lived nearby and I had come much further. But she was wearing a really short, sexy skirt and that more than made up for her tardiness. I asked her what she was drinking and she ordered a soda. I was sad she didn't seem much like a partier, but I figured it wasn't gonna ruin my night, so I kept the drinks coming.

Despite her hot skirt (and cute face) I felt like we didn't have a whole lot in common. I mean, I'm well traveled. I have an interesting family. I'm into gam-

bling and drinking whiskey and hard rock and roll. *She,* on the other hand, seemed kinda tame. She was into knitting and afternoon tea. I may have just been wasted, but I think at one point she said something about liking to watch fish swim. I feel like she would have been better suited to date someone like my grandmother.

So I pulled out one of my fail-safe tricks to get her disinterested. I yanked out a calculator at the bar once the check came and told her that, because I'm a gentleman, I'd pay for 10 percent more of the tab. She seemed appalled, which is exactly what I wanted, and I never heard from her again.

The night was actually a win/win for me. I got to have drinks with a pretty lady, but didn't have to make a big speech when I realized she wasn't right for me. My buddy Dave was pretty pissed at me for acting like such an ass, but I guess that's just the price you pay for getting out of an awkward situation.

## WHERE DID IT GO SO WRONG?

Their first physical impressions (and their mutual friend) led them both to be-lieve there might be some chemistry, but that's what dates are for: to unravel personalities and quirks and see if what might appear to be chemistry has any basis.

On Diane's end, it sounds like she merely thought their differences were interesting; he was an adventurous drinker and she, a slower-paced near tee-totaler. He liked traveling, she liked whale watching. What's wrong with that? Opposites sometimes *do* attract. However, the attraction obviously has to be

mutual. When people are putting on their best faces on a first date, it's tough to decipher whether or not there's potential – and the answer might be very different for each perspective partner.

One thing *is* for sure: it's never good to assume the guy is going to pick up a check on the first date (or *any* date) just because he's a guy. Yeah, yeah, we can go on about old-fashioned manners and chivalry, but that doesn't mean it's a safe bet. That said, Diane made it clear she wasn't upset about splitting the bill. Instead, it was the tacky way in which Caleb determined their percentages that turned her completely off.

Caleb, by behaving in such an irritating, passive-aggressive way, contributed to the collective women's belief that men are all idiots. Instead of just enjoying their time together and simply sending an email conveying something like, "I had a good time and although I don't feel there was a connection, I'd love to stay in touch," he had some silly elaborate plan (complete with props!) to get her off his back. Lame.

What I *will* give Caleb credit for is that he recognized early on that Diane wasn't his type. And while he could have tried to get her into bed and *then* pulled his lame-ass stunt to get her disinterested, he refrained from leading her on. (We're giving him the benefit of the doubt here. Had she gotten tipsy, he might have made that move.)

And hey, let's give Diane this: She did at least bail after Caleb produced a calculator from his baggy Gap jeans. Some women would have overlooked such tackiness because of being blinded by Caleb's good looks, but Diane was wise enough to see this as a pretty strange red flag. Silver lining? At least he didn't pull out an abacus.

"You're about as easy as a nuclear war."

– Duran Duran

I am about to admit something I probably shouldn't, but here goes: I found myself crying last week at a Sylvan Learning Center commercial. You know the one; the kid has trouble in school so his parents enroll him in this learning center to help him learn to read better. He gets his report card and proudly shows his mom that he got straight A's. She beams with pride.

It gets worse. The previous week, I had cried when I heard the song "Gold Digger" by Kanye West. I like the song, so I know they weren't tears of contempt. But I heard the lyrics, "If you ain't no punk, holla we want pre-nup!" and my eyes welled up with tears. I think (and I'm not kidding when I say this) these were tears of pure joy. I was so moved by the talent exemplified in this rap song; I could not prevent my emotion from just spilling out.

I mentioned this to a male friend of mine, and after staring at me blankly for what seemed like 20 minutes, he finally asked, "Wait … WHAT?"

I repeated, "Yes, I cried during the rap song 'Gold Digger' and I'm really not sure why …"

"Is it because you're crazy?"

That settled *that* conversation. But the question is: *does* that make me crazy? And if so, is it beyond my control? Although some men are quite emotional, why is it that most of them have the ability *not* to cry at *Snoopy Come Home* and many women (myself included) cry for weeks? Is it our brains, our upbringing or a perfect mixture of both?

Yeah, yeah, we've all heard it before: men and women are different. Some argue that it's completely biochemical while others blame the chasm between genders on rearing. But my theory is this: ya know how women get two X's for sex chromosomes and men get an X and a Y? I think that little tiny strip of DNA that's missing from the Y chromosome contains the ability to remember *not* to sleep with your girlfriend's best friend.

Granted, I'm no doctor. (Although I do have a bachelor degree in psych with a concentrated study in neuropsych.) And while my missing-piece theory may or may not be true, scientists *do* believe both the "nature" and "nurture" camps are right – there are of course biological differences between guys and girls that account for some of our behavior, and then some of it is a result of the way in which the people who shape our lives (i.e. parents, teachers, peers) influence us.

We know all of this because by now it has become ingrained in our psyches because of countless books and articles about men and women having a different biological make-up. Now remember, this isn't an exact science. There's little I hate more than a hack comedian who gets on stage sipping his (or her) stupid comedy juice while saying shit like: "Women … love to shop! And men, they hate it! Women can't get enough chocolate. Men, they just want sex … blah, blah, blah." It's boring, lazy comedy and it makes me uncomfortable even talking about it.

That said (and I do hate to admit this) there are some truths to the stereotypes. Not *all* of them, of course, and everyone is unique, but as a collective whole, yeah some of this stuff is founded. While I'm going to give some broad strokes regarding biological make-up, I want to stress that this isn't meant to be a scientific book about gender. There are doctors and scientists far more qualified than me (at least I hope there are) to discuss such things. Where *my* expertise comes in is that I've been broken up with more times than I'd care to count and I've decided to try and find out the science behind it. So the focus of the next chapter is: with the knowledge that our brains and bodies and perceptions make us different from the other gender, how do we go through the cycle of relationships?

# CHAPTER 2

# Wired That Way

The brain matters – quite literally. More specifically, the amount of white matter and gray matter in the male vs. female human brain differ, which could very well contribute to some differences in processing skills. Psychologist Richard Haier of U.C. Irvine (as well as other neuropsychologists from New Mexico) conducted a study where they concluded that women have 10 times the amount of white matter in their brains as men, whereas men have about 6.5 times the amount of gray matter as women. (Carey, Bjorn, et al. "Men and Women Really Do Think Differently," *Live Science Journal*, January, 2005.)

In this article, one of the study's co-authors, Rex Jung, theorized that this variation in white/gray matter could be why men and women seem to take in information differently. He concluded that men seem better at "localized processing," (Carey gives the example of mathematics) while women are better (in Carey's words) "at integrating and assimilating information … which aids language skills."

We'll come back to all of this, but I'll tell you right now it *doesn't* mean that women can't be great at math or men, fabulous speakers. Of course they can. What it does reiterate is that to have any hope of understanding the opposite sex, we'd better pay some attention in bio-chem class.

I remember the first time I ever learned there might be an actual physical difference in the male vs. female brain. I'd read an article that illustrated how a part of the limbic system that partially regulates emotion and some verbal perception was actually larger in the average female brain than in the male's. I don't recall the exact source, but I do remember (for some reason) jumping up and down, excitedly showing my guy friends the article while shouting: "Look, *see* guys? You *are* a-holes." This, of course, doesn't mean that men have no capacity to be emotional or perceptive or that they are in fact, a-holes. (Also, when bragging, I conveniently ignored the part of the article that talked about males allegedly having stronger reasoning skills.)

Maybe you're thinking, "Who cares about math or vocabulary or crying at movies? How does this all relate to sex or guys who cheat or hysterical women?" (And maybe, for all I know, you're thinking about New York cheesecake.) If it is sex on your mind, well hey … let's talk about that first.

**SEX**

## RAGING HORMONES

It's not just squishy brain matter that makes a difference between genders. The human endocrine system produces hormones, and while both men and women have "male" (i.e. testosterone) and "female" (i.e. estrogen) sex hormones, the one is higher in guys and the other is higher in chicks. As a rule (and it's not a rule I love, nor is it always the case), higher amounts of testosterone lead to a higher sex drive. This helps explain why a woman might claim to have a headache when a guy is trying to remove her pants. Sometimes it's easier to fake a physical ailment than to admit, "Hey, I'm just not feeling it right now." (This, in my experience, is an excuse that many men simply can't fathom.)

But there are also emotional reasons for differences – not necessarily in sex drive itself, but in the way in which we view sex. Because many men, as we mentioned earlier, are wired to process information and stimuli locally, (some

call this compartmentalizing) they can focus on sex just for the physical sake of having sex. Women, on the other hand, integrate and assimilate information (and this could possibly include past memories of arguments or hurt feelings), which can make it tougher to just "let go." It might seem odd that the amount and type of brain matter can make a difference in how we see sex, but it can. Again, this may have less to do with physical *drive* and more to do with how we process our emotions and memories.

Sometimes it's just a matter of us being turned on by different things. Maybe, due to hormonal differences, women just don't *want* it as much as men do. Maybe they *do* … but just not with the guy who wants it with them. And for some, it really is about the chase. Are you wired to always want for something more? Does it become boring once you know you can have it? That's pretty common, for both genders. It often has to do with emotional and mental blocks caused by our memories, which keep us from exploring healthier relationships. We'll talk about this more later on.

## CAN'T SPELL "EVOLVE" WITHOUT "LOVE"

We're gonna continue to explore the differences between sex drives, but let's for a moment get back to a basic question: Assuming you agree that lots of men are prone to lying, let's ask: why *do* men lie? Is there an evolutionary advantage to fibbing if you're a guy? Did a caveman have to make up excuses because he had been grunting over some naked chick he eyeballed in the forest? "Hey baby, I'm sorry I'm late bringing this saber-tooth tiger home, but … I … um, I … totally got stuck in some quicksand. It's madness out there. Now give me some lovin'."

And has it helped the women who have chosen to let their emotions take over, as opposed to reacting more calmly? "You can take your saber-tooth tiger and shove it. GET OUT OF MY CAVE."

This isn't about pointing fingers. It's about digging a little deeper into who we really are and how the opposite sex *perceives* us. The answer to whether or not our wiring (which leads to our actions) is evolutionary is … in short, yeah, it *has* to be. Evolutionary theory has taught us that those species fitted to their environment survive. And in order to do that and thrive as a species, we have to procreate. From the dawn of *Homo sapiens*, man has had to spread his seed. And now in modern times, women have more of a choice than ever before as to whose seed they choose. Are they gonna want the guy who's obviously ogling every waitress they see or do they choose the man who says: "No, baby, I wasn't looking at her boobs. You're the only boobs I see."

Bam, the man lied to get laid. Was there another, perhaps better, choice? Sure. But lying in these kinds of cases seems to work, has always worked and will probably continue to work. The lying "fit" survive to spread their seed.

So back to that limbic system. It's a pretty old part of the brain and the fact that parts of it seem to have evolved differently in the male vs. female brain might suggest that we are evolving in different ways for a reason. There are so many theories as to what emotion *is* and what it *means* that if we talked about them all, this would be a very different book. I think, however, it is safe to say that men view women as more emotional than they are. But why, from a more philosophical standpoint, might that be true?

Here's one important factor. Obviously, the way we're wired is also due to the way we're brought up. Boys (in most societies) are discouraged from showing their emotions. Therefore, after time they get conditioned to show them less. "Be a man," they might hear, or: "Stiff upper lip" or the universal: "Crying is for girls." If girls heard the same thing from their peers (and parents) over and over in response to showing emotion, they too might hold back a bit more. Both genders sometimes feel sadness or love or passion, but one gender might be more likely to let it all out.

To help illustrate the point of conditioning, I've had a tendency to want to repeatedly drive by an ex-boyfriend's house after he breaks up with me. Over time, I've learned that this doesn't get me the guy back, but it *does* get me the reputation of being a "psycho-bitch." Therefore, over time, I've been conditioned to *not* conduct (as many) drive bys as I might have in the past.

One of my main beefs with books about the anatomy of the male vs. female brain is that we can usually find whatever we *want* to find. If I come up with a hypothesis that women do *this* and men do *that* based on brain structure, I can almost guarantee I'll find literature to support it. For example, if I wanted to prove that women process their emotions in a more efficient way than men, there are tons of studies that make this conclusion. But I could just as easily try to prove that men are better at using the logical portions of their brains and therefore handle their emotions better. The question becomes: "What is 'better' or 'more efficient'?" That's why, while I noted some main structural differences in the brain, I think it's just as vital to discuss perception.

## WHAT'S UNDER THAT SUPER-EGO?

The infamous psychoanalyst Sigmund Freud may have focused much of his work on the belief that we're almost completely motivated by the penis (women want one, he claimed, and men want what they have to be bigger and better), but sex isn't *everything*. (Gasp, crowd boos!)

Although he was far from being the only analyst to espouse the following, Freud made famous the idea that we have thoughts buried deep below the conscious mind. These are the memories and emotions (both positive and negative) we have pushed into what I call the "dark places." Freud basically said they rear their heads through dreams, slips of the tongue and deep analysis through such means as word-association games.

With regard to slips, (a.k.a. Freudian slips), here's an example: I was once having "relations" with a guy and I *meant* to say: "I love you," but instead said: "I love that vampire guy from *Twilight*." (Longest Freudian slip *ever*.) Probably not the best time for my subconscious to pop up and express itself, but we've all slipped up verbally. Whether this is because of something that's bubbling up from deep within or it just happens with no real reason is not entirely known.

What I will say is you can tell a lot about someone by how they make associations (or as I call them, *leaps*). Because guys and women have different points of view, they're probably gonna take different leaps when associating thoughts.

Let's play a game. Go get yourself a writing utensil and in the blanks next to the following words, write down the *first* word that comes to mind. Don't over-think it. Just write whatever immediately comes into your head. Ready?

**Spaghetti:**  _____

**Rocket:**  _____

**Car:**  _____

**Man:**  _____

**Triangle:**  _____

**Internet:**  _____

**Foreplay:**  _____

**Woman:**  _____

**Sex:**  _____

**Share:**  _____

**Foursome:**  _____

I asked a couple of my friends (one male, one female) to play this game. Here are their results:

| DANNY | | CARLY | |
|---|---|---|---|
| Spaghetti: | Food | Spaghetti: | Full |
| Rocket: | Fast | Rocket: | Moon |
| Car: | Yes | Car: | Travel |
| Man: | Strong | Man: | Fight |
| Triangle: | Bongos | Triangle: | Hole |
| Internet: | Porn | Internet: | Shopping |
| Foreplay: | Porn | Foreplay: | Kissing |
| Woman: | Pretty | Woman: | Milk |
| Sex: | Me | Sex: | Kid |
| Share: | MILF | Share: | Cooperation |
| Foursome: | Golf | Foursome: | Oh s$#%, is he trying to get me to do *that* again? |

Take a look at your answers and compare them to my buddies'. While it's not possible to interpret these answers objectively, it's kind of fun to compare this male vs. female sampling.

For example, in the case of Carly, it would seem that the original words inspire more of what the item those words represent are used for. Spaghetti makes her full; one takes a rocket to the moon. The interesting association in her case I believe is the word "sex" which she associates with "kid." (Well, not so much interesting to us as it might be to her boyfriend.)

It doesn't take Freud to analyze Danny's responses. The most telling was his response to "sex" in which the first word that came to his mind was "me." (I guess he has fun with himself on cold winter nights.) And while Carly took the word "share" to be associated with "cooperation," Danny apparently thought this meant the pop diva "Cher" who, it would seem, is a mother he'd like to ... ya know.

The words "Internet," "foreplay" and "four-some" inspired very telling responses from both genders. Note that for Danny, the word-associations for "Internet" and "foreplay" are the same word, and it's not "girlfriend."

While it's tough to find empirical meaning in this game, word associations can be pretty revealing. In fact, many advertisers use them in focus groups when trying out new marketing ideas. Ask a few of your friends to play and see if you can find any differences with the patterns.

All right, so enough talk about the biological and psychoanalytical theories behind gender differences. Let's get to the part where we figure out what to actually *do* about those differences.

"Don't know if I saw you if I would kiss you or kill you; it probably wouldn't matter to you anyhow."

– Bob Dylan

The first time I tried online dating, I got an email within five minutes of posting my profile. It was from a guy who called himself "Hot-pants 560," and luckily for all of us, I saved the email and would like to share:

> *"Dear Indie-lover 100 (I like indie music; what of it?)*
>
> *I read profile and think you pretty lady. I want to take you to dis-*
> *cothèque in big city. I would like to make dancing with you. We could*
> *do tango or the robot-dance.*
> *Please to email me as possibly as soon. Keep smiling pretty eyes.*
>
> *Love always, Hot-pants 560"*

My favorite part of the email was his declaration to *always* love me. Why wouldn't he, right? And while the broken English wasn't so much an issue, I was concerned that he thought doing the robot dance would be a fine way

to spend a first (or any) date. I bring this up not to discourage folks from using online dating (which we'll discuss later) but to share that no matter what your hunting techniques are for finding a date, they are not fail-safe. This of course is not to say that I *didn't* accept Hot-pants 560's offer to "make dancing" with him, but … well … I think it's best if we don't talk more about it.

For many of us, the search for the perfect guy or girl starts early. For me, it was probably, oh, kindergarten when the soft, full lips of Davy Jones (*The Monkees*, not *Pirates of the Caribbean*) caught my six-year-old eye. I saw his gentle features and heard the English accent and BOOM … the search was on. (Just an aside, I used to fantasize that Davy would fall down a manhole and I, being still six and all, would rescue him somehow and convince him to live with me in my room in Waco, Texas. I had this dream every night and I'm sad to report it hasn't happened yet.)

But since this crush, I've been hunting endlessly for the man to fill Davy's tiny shoes. Maybe we've all been on the hunt since our first real crushes. And if you're like many of us, you've tried it all: bars, blind dates, the Internet, gay bathhouses … (Wait, that last one was a typo.)

I've even tried meeting guys at dog parks, without having a dog with me (and I realize that might sound creepy). A few years ago I recall trying to lock eyes with a cute blonde who had a basset hound he called "Angela." (And yeah, it took me awhile to get the Angela Bassett reference.) I smiled at the guy and his response was to look horrified, scoop up Angela and leave the park. Excellent.

In this next chapter we're gonna explore the ways in which many of us search for love (or sex … or perhaps just a single date). I'll give some pros and cons of different approaches and compare how boys and girls go about their own personal hunts.

# CHAPTER 3

# The hunt

Let's just start with the obvious: males are born to hunt. I hate actually saying that because a) it's trite and b) some men use it to justify their bad behavior. But it seems this trait goes back to the beginning and can't be ignored. Some believe these hunting instincts might cause a man to lose interest in a woman he's been pursuing once he "gets" her. While we women might not find solace in the idea that our broken-hearted "How can he *do* this to me?" questions might be reduced to animalistic instincts, this is a possibility we must at least consider.

But what about women? Do we tend to cling to men (even the ones we know aren't right for us) out of an instinctual need to be protected? I don't say this to set back the feminist movement; I, for one, believe women are bright and independent and tough as nails when we need to be. However, I admit that while I pride myself on being intelligent, I *can* be clingier than the average guy, even with the knowledge that I can take care of myself. Now, I'm not referring to being taken care of financially or even sexually. I'm talking about literal *protection*. Does this reflect itself in *my* hunting? If so, how would it explain my tendency to be attracted to skinny "pretty boys?" (Also,

I'm kind of doubting that little cutie-pie Davy Jones could have shielded me from, say a polar bear.)

In modern times, the ways in which men and women meet the opposite sex, despite our contrasting instinctual impulses, have become more similar to one another. And while we have been talking in generalities (and will continue to do so), I should probably mention that many women enjoy "the hunt," while lots of guys are monogamists. Whether we are fighting our natural instincts or merely evolving is up for debate.

## RIPE FOR HUNTING

### PUBBING IT

The local pub has always been a popular place to meet the opposite sex. Many people will tell you this is not a great location, because of both the possibility of beer-goggling and the lack of character reference for the person you're meeting. That said, I personally think bars are a fine place to meet, just as long as you're smart about it and don't get into a stranger's creepy van. (Also, it's probably not too bright to be so toasted you can't see the face of the person you're hitting on.)

Meeting people in bars can be a different experience depending on where you live. For example, unlike in the United States, many of my friends in the UK claim guys don't usually mosey on up to "birds" and buy them drinks. Instead they drink with their pals until the pub closes and the lights come on, at which point they try to leave with the cutest girl there. (These might actually just be the tactics of *my* English friends, as opposed to Englishmen in general, as many of them haven't had girlfriends in about 15 years.)

**HERE ARE A FEW RULES FOR MEN WHEN PICKING UP WOMEN IN BARS:**

1. **Don't hit on women who look like they might have a pimp waiting for them outside.** Usually, when it comes to relationship potential, those situations don't end well.

2. **As my friend Mike often says, "Chill-ax."** There's no need to list off every achievement you've ever received when first meeting a girl. Remember you're hitting on a woman, not trying to get into Harvard. (Unless the woman's name is "Harvard." Boom!)

3. **Ask to exchange emails instead of phone numbers.** Some women might think this shows a lack of commitment, but in reality it's easier to begin communication via the Internet than on the phone. (That way, you can never call too late or too early or have a coughing attack the minute you're leaving a voicemail.)

 **AND NOW SOME RULES FOR WOMEN WHEN MEETING MEN IN BARS:**

1. **If a guy seems totally wasted (and believe me, you can usually tell) do not give him your phone number.** Actually, even if he's sober, give him an email address you normally use for contests or spam. In other words, give him an address on an account you'd be happy to delete if need be.

2. **Don't give a stranger (no matter how cute he might be) too much information about yourself up front.** Unfortunately we can't trust everyone we meet and since you won't know this guy from Adam, it's better to play it safe.

3. **Don't let a guy you've just met walk you to your car/subway/ home.** Again, it's not safe until you know more about him. If you *do* plan to set up a date, you should initially meet him somewhere rather than have him pick you up.

I know I seem like an overprotective mom on this stuff, but we all have to be wary when meeting new potential partners. Rules aside, it's okay to enjoy the company of some cute new guy (or lady) showing you attention at a bar. But remember that whole thing about people sometimes lying or being coo-coo crazy? Yeah, be smart about who you pick up. If you give them too much information too quickly, you can't decide to take it back later.

## THE SET-UP

How many times have you had a friend or co-worker say: "Have I got the *perfect* mate for you?!" And how many times has that so-called "perfect mate" looked like a gargoyle (albeit a very sweet or smart gargoyle) on the top of a French library? It makes you wonder how your friends see *you* when they set you up with, say … a hobo who hangs out in the alley of the local Starbucks. "Does my friend think *I'm* a hobo?" you might ask, "… or does she just think I should settle?" (Please note: I'm not judging hobos here.)

Going on a date set up by a friend can be tricky and ego busting, but it really can be a good way to meet someone. For one, you have a reference who can hopefully assure you that your date for the night is not a crazed maniac. Second, it automatically gives you and your semi-stranger of a date something in common. (For example, if your friend Brian set you up, you can say stuff like: "Brian is such a D-bag sometimes, isn't he? But hey … we love him!")

**A FEW RULES FOR THE BLIND DATE:**

1. **Have your mutual friend email both parties a recent (and non-glamour-shot) photo of the other.** That way, there will be less surprise upon meeting and it will be less likely that one of you will scream, "Holy S$%^! Brian didn't *tell* me you look like k.d. lang!"

2. **Probably best not to bash your mutual friend too much.** Sure it's okay to mock a little (or, of course, say wonderful things) but if things don't work out, you don't want to risk any nastiness getting back to your pal.

3. **If the date *is* successful and there are subsequent dates, try not to give the setter-upper too many details about the relationship.** This might make him/her uncomfortable. (For example, perhaps you *shouldn't* say: "Hey Brian, I had the best sex ever last night with that co-worker of yours. Thanks for that!"

## VIRTUAL ROMANCE

As you may have surmised from my story regarding "Hot-Pants 560," meeting people online doesn't always go smoothly. But don't let "Hot-Pants" scare you into thinking it can *never* work. In fact in these modern times I know at least five couples who met online and then proceeded to have long-term relationships – some even getting married.

I've found that dating can be a numbers game. It's not a bad idea to cast a wide net, see what's out there and then, after reeling 'em in, choosing the most appropriate and exciting match for you. The fact that we live in a time when we can cast that net from our living rooms makes it all the better.

Here are a few things to keep in mind when meeting in cyberspace.

### A FEW RULES FOR INTERNET DATING:

1. **As with meeting a stranger in a bar, don't give up too much information too quickly.** Remember, no matter how many emails have been traded back and forth, you don't really *know* the person at the other end of the computer. (For all you know, the 35-year-old male doctor living in Manhattan might just be a 14-year-old young girl from Guam. Or, for that matter, it might be a creepy 60-year-old who was just released from prison.)

2. **While it's fun to flirt back and forth via email for awhile, don't wait too long before using the phone or (gasp) meeting up in person.** I'm not suggesting you rush a meeting, but the longer you send emails before meeting, the more expectation you build in your mind. (I remember sharing about 50 wonderful emails with a guy, but when he called his voice was so light and childlike, I actually thought he was Michael Jackson, may he rest in peace.)

3. **Trust your instincts!** If something strikes you as creepy or off-putting in someone's profile or emails, tread very carefully. There are a lot of wackos out there and the Internet is a fabulous playground for them. You might not even know what exactly is creeping you out, but remember that instincts have evolved for a reason, and listen to them.

## SETTING UP YOUR PROFILE:

Look, we all want to put our best feet forward when dating, and that can be tough when we have merely one page to describe ourselves. It's important that you be honest in your profiles. No, you don't have to say stuff like, "I get a lot of cold-sores in the winter" or "I will cut you in your sleep!" (Actually, if it's the last one, you probably shouldn't date for awhile.) But you should have at least one updated profile photo. (And hey, if you're 40, please don't put pictures up from your prom. Unless you graduated high school at 39.)

A lot of dating sites will ask you to write a headline or "tagline" for your profile. I think mine was something like "If you can't beat 'em, tie 'em up at least." I wasn't exactly going for an S & M statement. I did, however, want to get across that I was clever and sexy and perhaps don't take it all so seriously. (Side note: Unfortunately, I did get contacted by a few guys who were severely into leather.)

It's difficult to capture your essence in just a few paragraphs, but perhaps this will help: Ask yourself what is the first adjective that comes to mind when you think about you. Do you find yourself hilarious? Are you the most loyal person you know? Now I refuse to get too self-helpy here, so I'll just say go with your gut instinct. If an awesome sense of humor is what gives you confidence, then write something witty (or at least more clever than *my* tagline.)

When writing about your interests, there's no reason to list every band, movie or book you've ever loved. I always found it a bit off-putting when a guy listed hundreds of movies he deemed worthy. Not everyone feels this way, but to me the person who chooses to list a thousand of his favorite folk bands might have just a bit too much time to spare. Plus, because it's so easy to dismiss someone online, you don't want to hand your potential soul mate a reason to hit the "Next profile" button. (Like if I saw a guy who claimed he loves listening to Hannah Montana songs, I'd hit "Next" and I might miss out on a great guy. Or I might miss out on a Jonas brother.)

With regard to profile pictures, please try to avoid photos that have ex-girlfriends or ex-boyfriends in the shot. This includes the ones in which you have clearly cut out the ex. We can still see the arm around your waist or shoulder in the photo, and there's no reason to start a potential relationship with jealousy. Let's face it: our exes are our baggage. Why would you want to display a photo of what I call your "suitcase of crazy?" Believe me, your potential partner is gonna find all of that crazy soon enough, without your assistance.

## WORKING IT

Some people will tell you the office romance is taboo. While it can lead to problems (and is even prohibited in many workplaces), it can also be loads of fun. Plus, now instead of regarding it as your boring 40-hour workweek, you can think of it as your fun 40-hour getting-to-know-the-cute-Human-Resources-guy week.

While I mention this as an option, I should point out the difference between dating and having an affair. I never condone infidelity, but even if you're both single, you should note that office flings don't always become office relationships. It's important that everyone involved understands the parameters so there are fewer hard feelings if it doesn't work out. Trust me, you haven't felt scorn until you've f-ed over the office manager at your place of business.

If you *do* decide to spice up your work life with a casual, consensual fling, there are a few important guidelines you should consider:

1. **Sexual harassment isn't taken lightly in the workplace (or any-where, for that matter) so make sure the flirtation is two sided before making a move.** (FYI, harassment can go both ways, so if you're a woman hitting on a guy at work, you must be careful he feels the same way.)

2. **Even if the sexual chemistry is mutual, you should probably steer clear of hooking up with subordinates, particularly those directly beneath you.**

3. **If you're keeping it at the "fling" level, make sure it stays on the down low.** Part of the fun in a 2:00 PM rendezvous in the copy room is that you're doing it secretly. Also, remember what happened with that whole Bill Clinton/Linda Tripp/Monica gross-blue-dress deal? (If you're too young, look it up.) If that taught us nothing else, it proved that sometimes our work "friends" can't be trusted.

I once somewhat seriously dated a guy I worked with. Granted, we were dorm-resident advisors in college, but nonetheless, we saw each other every day in boring meetings, floor inspections, etc. When he dumped me for the R.A. on the 4th floor, I was mortified. (Mind you, that girl wore Jellies shoes and culottes.) And continuing to work with him every day after the breakup was not easy. (Although I will tell you that I saw the "other woman" recently at a college reunion and she *still* wears Jellies, which made me feel better.)

I mention this as a warning. While the workplace can be a great way to spark a romance, the risks are high that you'll eventually find yourself in some awkward situations. If you feel you're ready to take the leap into a real office relationship, there is a whole other set of rules you might want to think about:

1. **Make sure it's the real deal before taking the leap.** You could save each other a lot of heartache if you're honest with one another before beginning your relationship. Of course, you never know where a romance might take you, but if you know it *won't* go anywhere, don't take the plunge.

2. **Find out your workplace's rules for interoffice dating.** Some places ask that you disclose your relationship once it gets semi-serious. Some (although these days this is pretty rare) are adamantly against dating a coworker. If that is the case and you feel like the woman or man you're dating is worth it, one of you might have to consider finding a new job. Most likely dating is technically *allowed*, but frowned upon.

3. **Don't date someone at the office who might leave you for a ho-bag who wears Jellies.** I'm just sayin'…

## HERE COMES THE BRIDE …
## AND ALL HER CUTE WEDDING GUESTS

While there are lots of other fine places in which to prowl for the opposite sex (like perhaps church pews or school) my personal favorite place to meet a potential partner is at a friend's wedding. This is like speed dating with an open bar, especially if your friend is kind enough to seat you at a hot singles' table. (Personally, I always seem to get seated with married couples and their babies, which is why I've stopped buying people wedding gifts.)

Now let me please share a little tale to illustrate what *not* to do at a friend's wedding: body shots off a stranger on the dance floor. Yep, when my buddy Billy got married, I had a bit of a meltdown (as per usual) when I saw yet another ex-boyfriend enter the room with his new fiancée, who cattily I must mention was wearing a formal gown over jeans. I guess perhaps I'd had one too many tequila shots (if there is such a thing) and I set my sights on a gorgeous guy at the bar. One thing led to another and next thing I know, I was lifting my dress and letting him pour lemon drops on my ankles while simultaneously licking them off.

Tacky. Needless to say, I'm no longer friends with Billy and things didn't really work out with gorgeous-guy (but we'll discuss him more in another chapter). That aside, the romantic setting in which your friend is expressing his or her undying love to a life-partner can set a beautiful tone for your own relationship. So before you toss that wedding invite, think again. But keep these things in mind:

1. **If you're close enough to the bride-and-groom to be, let them know you are in fact single.** I mean you don't want to make it all about you or anything (so don't be obnoxious about it), but it's certainly okay to mention that you're looking and you would possibly prefer to be seated at the hot singles' table instead of the married-couples-with-babies table.

2. **If you do meet someone attractive, try your best not to make out at the wedding.** You don't want to steal the spotlight from the couple whose union you're actually supposed to be celebrating. (In other words, don't do what I did.)

3. **Along the lines of rule #2, if you actually meet someone with whom you might later want to date, try not to get plastered.** Yeah, yeah, weddings are for getting a *little* drunk, but sometimes when we're toasted, what we think is charming is actually a turn-off. Make sure to at least eat a few dinner rolls so you can soak up some of that champagne.

## WHERE "NOT" TO HUNT

So we've talked about some good places for men and women to meet potential romantic partners. How 'bout we scroll through a few places that should *not* be on that list:

## PRISON

I don't care how sexy you think someone's snake tattoo is, I strongly advise you not to start up a relationship with someone in prison. I understand that people in jail need love too, but the last thing anyone who's looking for a healthy relationship needs is an inmate writing them love letters.

I realize there are some people (mostly women) who seek out partners they can "fix" or "save." And I'm not saying some of these men can't eventu-

ally change their ways, but they're going to need to work on their own self-rehabilitation before they're capable of sharing their romantic love with *you*. Plus, they might just be hitting you up for cigarette money.

## FAMILY REUNIONS

I'd think this one was pretty obvious and self-explanatory, but just in case: avoid trying to pick someone up at a family gathering. Most likely, you're related (hence, the whole *family* aspect of it) so yeah, unless you're Jerry Lee Lewis, it's probably not a good idea.

## CAN'T SPELL FUNERAL WITHOUT "FUN"

Out of respect for those grieving, it's probably best not to hit on someone at a funeral service or wake. I'm sure people have met this way (and it probably makes for a good story) but I find it normally upsets the balance. And when I say: "I find," really what I mean is: "I found out" when I tried once to make "sexy eyes" with a rabbi at a gravesite.

## SEX ADDICTS ANONYMOUS MEETING

I can't tell you how many times I've heard of people trying to date out of SA meetings. I know a woman (let's call her Dora) who claimed to be a sex and love addict and would regularly attend meetings. Subsequently, Dora met and slept with over 50 guys (and a few ladies) from said meetings, (including at least two different sponsors). I'm not mocking her; this really happened. Sadly, sometimes bringing like minds (and like sex drives) together can lead to mischief. Putting a bunch of sex/love addicts in one big circle is like sticking a porn addict in the Hustler store. Speaking of …

## SEX-TOY SHOP

Lastly, unless you're enormously into sex toys and dirty magazines, you might not wish to meet your possible mate in an adult sex shop. *"Why the F not?"* you might ask. While you might have some built-in conversation over the vibrating eggs, this could set your relationship up to be totally sex based, and if you're looking for something more you might end up disappointed. This isn't to say it's *impossible* to meet someone in this fashion, but sex shops are usually better to go to once you're already involved.

---

All this does not mean that you should begin hanging out in bars for the sole purpose of trying to meet the love of your life, or for that matter, that you will not meet your future spouse at a family reunion. It's good to try different approaches and see what feels the most comfortable. If something isn't working (like say, online dating) try to get someone to arrange a blind date. You'll know what feels comfortable for you, and if nothing ever does … welcome to the magical world of dating!

"All lies and jest, still, a man hears what he wants to hear and disregards the rest."

– Simon and Garfunkel

In my experience, when I've met someone with whom I spark, it's usually because he's very, *very* wrong for me. I realize this might sound cliché and many of us might feel they have the same issue. But I'm telling you, my "chooser" has been completely off.

Let's see, there was the guy who I met coming out of the West Hollywood Gay and Lesbian Center, (he claimed he was just using their bathroom). Then there was the born-again Evangelical who told me in no uncertain terms I was going to suffer eternal damnation. (Yep, slept with him for over a year.) There was the guy who collected dolls (and yeah, I've listened to "Free to Be, You

and Me" many times and know it's okay for boys to have dolls – just not necessarily 5000 of them.) Oh, and let's not forget the man who constantly tried
to set me up with his other friends … *while we were dating.* And yet I pursued
these men, and in some cases even fell madly in love with them.

These men (and there are many, many more) were waving their bright
red flags so high I was like a bull in a bullfight I was bound to lose. So what
made me fall for them again and again? Was there some sort of link they had
in common that might illustrate a clear pattern? Yep … they were all really
funny. (Well, all of them except the guy who liked to go dancing at gay dance
clubs. He was just really pretty.)

So bingo. Humor is and always has been my Achilles' heel, and no matter how many red flags a man might have waved in front of me, they were
obscured by my apparent need for a good laugh. For me, this pattern goes all
the way back to childhood. When my mom read me fairytales, I was less interested in the glass slipper from the prince and more interested in the guy sell-
ing the glass slipper in order to fund his stand-up comedy career. My mother
tried to buy me a poster of John Travolta and I insisted we find a full-bodied
poster of comedian Charles Grodin circa 1978. (Apparently, there wasn't much
demand for such a thing, so I had to settle for a poster of Robin Williams
as "Mork." It took me an hour to cut out "Mindy" and replace her with my
second-grade class photo.)

But why? WHY must they always be funny? WHY HAVEN'T I BEEN ABLE
TO SETTLE FOR GORGEOUS AND RICH AND SMART? WHAT HAP-
PENED TO GRODIN'S TALK SHOW? WHY AM I YELLING? Maybe I can
trace it back to my mother choosing my very funny father as a mate. Maybe
that's what I learned love was supposed to be. Keep it light, keep it dry, keep
'em laughing and never get too emotionally involved. We see these patterns as
children and they help shape who we are and what we think we're looking for
later in life.

Ask yourself what your patterns are. Do you always go for the adventurous
type? Do you find yourself attracted to people with serious addictions? Some
of us are fixers and some of us play the victim. We've *learned* this … either
from our parents or from past experiences wherein our behavior and patterns
have paid off.

I used to argue with my therapist when she'd tell me, "Cecily, your chooser
is broken. We need to fix your chooser." I'd say, "Nope, I'm not choosing these

guys. *They're choosing me!*" But as I've learned and experienced more relation-ships, I realize that we always have a hand in the choosing. Maybe we are sought out by a certain type, but it's always in our power to accept or reject whatever relationships we want for ourselves. It took me awhile to figure out my pattern (just to reiterate: funny, doll-collecting, detached religious fanatics,) but once I did, it has helped free me to see that there are always other options.

## CHAPTER 4

# Fixing your chooser

Initial chemistry can be a tricky thing, especially when we have patterns that date back to our childhoods. We can be turned on or off by traits without understanding why. For example, the pitch of a person's voice or shade of his hair can literally make our hearts beat with lust or gross us out. (Granted, if a guy showed up sounding like either McGruff the Crime Dog or Fran Drescher, we'd probably have a right to take issue.)

Sometimes because of these subconscious built-in preconceptions, we might reject perfectly great relationship potential. I once met a guy online, but after talking to him on the phone, I determined that his voice was "too thick." On paper (or in our case, on the bytes that make up a computer program) he was pretty close to perfect: good-looking, smart, active, successful … but that voice: it was just so …"thick." My mom convinced me to give him a shot regardless, so begrudgingly, I did. And he actually turned out to be a pretty great guy.

However, I ultimately did end up rejecting him because he had what I believed to be an unhealthy appreciation for REO Speedwagon. (I mean, *really*?) Be that as it may, basing my attraction (or lack thereof) on the thickness of his voice was unfair and it would have been a shame if I hadn't at least given him a chance.

That being said, we can't deny that there is such a thing as chemistry. Some scientists believe that much of our physical response to one another is based on pheromones. If this is true, we can't deny these chemical triggers any more than we could deny that old milk smells bad. This might explain why sometimes we meet and feel an instant lust. (I've had this happen, but usually the guy has a guitar slung around his neck. So it could be pheromones or it could be that damn Les Paul. Gets me every time.)

Beyond the literal chemistry, you'll often hear guys claim they initially fall for a woman based on her looks. I'm not judging this; it makes sense. Men are turned on (usually more than women) by visual stimulation. But if you dig a little deeper, what *about* these looks exactly is making these guys fall? Is it the current culture's socially acceptable model of what is *supposed* to be considered hot (thin, blonde, big-boobed Barbie type)? Or, and perhaps slightly more disturbing, is it that men fall for women who either look like their mothers or like a caretaker or teacher they had deemed attractive when they were young kids? Usually we're not aware of what has created our "types." But if we think back far enough we can sometimes figure it out.

Same thing goes for women, but instead of visual stimulation, a lot of us base our attraction more on how a guy makes us feel. Do we feel protected, nervous, sexy or anxious when he's around? I can trace what I find attractive in a guy back to pre-school. (And yes, I was boy crazy even then.) Aside from Davy Jones, the first real boy to make my heart go a-flutter was funny (of course) and had a very calming effect on me. Granted we were only five, but I remember when all the other boys were running amok at recess, he made confident eye contact and told me my painting of a rainbow was "very good." (Actually, for the record, it was awful. But I appreciated the compliment.)

Well, it just so happened that he had blue eyes. And so I've always kind of had a thing for blue eyes. Could this be traced back to how that particular blue-eyed boy in pre-school made me *feel*? Am I always and forever trying to find *him*? Maybe. Or maybe I just respond visually to lighter eyeballs. But it makes sense that these kinds of early experiences (in this case with a funny five-year-old who had blue eyes) have helped shape my "type."

About eight years later, John Hughes didn't help matters when he cast Andrew McCarthy in "Pretty in Pink." The first time I saw him pop up in front of Molly Ringwald from behind that computer, my heart melted. This added to my blue-eye affinity, an obsession with dimples and anyone who might be named "Blane." Once we make that brain-heart connection (in my case, feeling nauseatingly excited when Blane invited Molly's character to the prom), it's tough to change it.

But how do we determine if our "choosers" are off or broken? Do you find yourself repeating the same relationship over and over, only to get less-than-healthy results? That might be a clue.

It helps to figure out just *why* you like who you like. Once you do, it might be liberating to consider that the people you meet now are not the same as the people you once had feelings for, even if they have the same eye color or the same taste in music. Each new person we encounter has his own individual set of behaviors, experiences, neurotransmitters and yes, pheromones, that completely differentiate him from all others. Now I know this might *seem* obvious, but our subconscious likes to play dirty tricks on us.

## CHOOSING FOR THE RIGHT REASONS

In first grade I brought a Star Wars trading card of Chewbacca to school. My brother had given it to me, and even at age six I knew I could use it as a manipulative tool to make boys like me. I slowly pulled the card (which, I believe, came with a very stale piece of pink gum) from my Monkees lunchbox and made sure the two boys who sat next to me (Kevin and David) noticed it.

My plan worked a little too well. For the four hours following my "Chewbacca reveal," both Kevin and David begged me to let them have it. And so I behaved in a way you'd think would have heralded a future Mae West. I gathered them around me at recess and said the following: "Boys? You can compete for my love for the rest of the week. Whoever serves me as the better boyfriend will have earned the Chewbacca card. May the best man win."

So for the next five days, Kevin and David vied for my love … because of their love for Chewbacca. They rushed to fetch my lunch tray in the cafeteria. They carried my book bags. I think Kevin even wrote me a song, which if I remember correctly was quite beautiful. (I mean, it was no "Last Train to Clarksville," but it was a nice effort.)

I liked them both and I absolutely could not decide which one to reward. But the point to this story is that at the age of six I was choosing a boy (so to speak) based on who was kinder to me. It's such a shame I couldn't carry that criterion with me for the rest of my life. At six it wasn't who was funnier or

who had the bluest eyes or who seemed the most like Charles Grodin. It was *who was kinder.* And when we're dealing with our "choosers," that's a pretty damn important decisive factor.

I truly can't remember whether Kevin or David won the card, but I'm pretty sure both guys blew me off once the competition was over. I didn't mind though, because I got to be fawned over for a short time, even if I did have to bribe them. I was just like a younger female version of Bret Michaels from "Rock of Love," except without all the booze and skanky hos. I've always said I was hip beyond my years.

## THE FACTOR OF FEAR

No doubt you've heard women say such things as: "He loves me, but he's just too scared to get into a serious long-term relationship." However, lots of people claim this is bullshit. They say a guy either likes you enough for a real relationship or he likes you only well enough to have you conveniently on hand when certain urges arise, and he acts on those feelings either way. While I can't disagree that this is sometimes true, and while we women certainly let some men get away with stringing us along, I believe there *is* such a thing as being too scared to put two feet in.

Usually it goes down like this: A man (for example) chases a woman he feels is playing hard to get. She's flattered but resists him until finally she relents and lets him in. After a few months of dating, he appears bored and wants out. Seems pretty straightforward … he liked her as a conquest but not as a human being and potential partner. In other words, he's just not that into her. Simple story, right? Sound familiar?

But *does* he choose to leave because he's not "into her?" Or is it possible that he's not truly comfortable with himself and therefore the idea of allowing her to see his true colors and scars, as begins to happen in the first few months, is terrifying? True, the "I'm just not ready for a relationship" line does sound like a B.S. cover for: "You're just not doing it for me," and I'm sure sometimes it is just that. But we can't completely disregard the possibility that when he says he's not ready, he might be onto something.

Hopefully it's clear that it's a good idea to feel healthy about yourself before deciding to share your life with another. Perhaps those who shy away from true, long-term intimacy just don't feel good enough about themselves, and that's why they are not yet prepared to shed their facades and get metaphorically naked. (Although if it's a guy we're talking about, getting naked isn't usually the problem.)

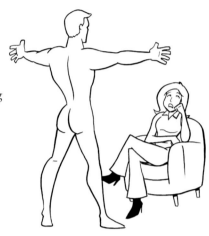

Why is this relevant? Because many of us seem to choose mates who end up running away and we kick ourselves, wondering what the reason might have been. However, we can find telltale signs of this reticence if we choose to look. For example, if a person comes on extra strong this can be an indication he's not ready for commitment. He's more interested in the chase, or at most the "honeymoon" period, because he doesn't want a woman to see anything beyond his surface personality. (The one he created in order to make girls swoon.)

I was once pursued for over a year by a guy we'll call John. He called every day, sent flowers and told me we were destined for one another. I finally gave in and went out with him. After we had been dating for a month, and just two days after we slept together, he called and said he was getting back together with his ex. It's hard for me to believe that he'd invest a *year* of his life chasing me, wanting only sex as his goal. He could easily have gotten laid; he was a good-looking, charming guy. Clearly (or at least it seems clear) he had some feelings of some sort toward me, and yet the minute we became intimate, he bolted. (Maybe I'm just really bad in bed, but let's assume that's not the case.)

Sometimes the commitment problem stems not from the person being afraid to show himself; it's that his expectations of you are out of control. This could have been the case with John. If someone puts you on a pedestal before really knowing you … yeah, that's a major red flag. Sure it can boost the ego a bit, but ask yourself: how can he really feel this intensely before he knows anything about me?

Some call this being addicted to the thrill of the chase; I call it "The Muffin-Top Theory." We all love the top part of a muffin, but when we get to the crumbly base, we toss it. (You might recall a *Seinfeld* episode about this very

subject.) Some people are interested in
only the top of the "muffin" because either
they don't want to see *your* base or because
they don't want you to see theirs. Either
way, watch for this behavior, especially if
you're prone to choosing people who come
on strong. As flattering as it might be to
get a lot of attention, he might be interested only in your … er, muffin top.

## RED FLAG/GREEN FLAG

I'm now going to share some stories of how some friends and I have met
people in the past. Your job is to see how good you are at spotting the potential danger cues that I (or my friends) either clearly missed or chose to ignore.
As you read these stories, see if you follow any of the same patterns. Maybe
you find yourself needing to "fix" or "control" or "be the victim." If that does
seem to be your standard, is it working?

## CENTER OF THE UNIVERSE

There's a guy sitting at a bar and he's snorting cocaine off a barstool … no
wait, that's too easy. Let's try again. There's a guy sitting at the bar and he
seems drunk, but in a charming, Dean Martin kind of way. He's super loud,
super hot, and seems to have a plethora of women around him. Yet I'm drawn
to him and he seems to feel the same, because when he's not receiving cheek
kisses from his female friends, he's staring right at me.

Once the sea of ladies parts, he stands up and walks toward the back of the
room where I'm sitting. He sits down (uninvited) at my table and says "Will
you please take me to Knott's Berry Farm?" My girlfriends giggle and flirt, but
he never averts his eyes from me.

See any red flags? Well perhaps not, although being surrounded by a
harem of women could be construed as a little "flaggy." But here's some
background that might put things into perspective. Another of my weaknesses

(besides going for the blue-eyed funny men) is that I tend to like the guy who has to take center stage: the quarterback, the lead singer, and my favorite, the class clown. And just because a man falls into this category does not make him a horrible human being; nor does it mean he will never find a wonderful woman to live the rest of his life with, happily.

The thing is, however, relationships with this type of man haven't worked for me. So, since I can observe his overconfidence immediately, I have to try to fight against the attraction. Why? Because the truth is, *I* like to have center stage. And yet I continue to go for these boisterous charmers –perhaps because I'm trying to live *my* life vicariously through these attention-craving, loved-by-all men. *If everyone adores HIM and I'm WITH him, they will adore me too.* The reality is quite different though; while everyone is paying attention to him, no one is paying attention to me. And I *like* attention.

Now, there isn't anything inherently wrong with going for the most popular guy. It just depends on your vantage point. If you have an ego that can withstand the attention heaped upon your partner (and ideally not a jealousy problem), go for it. Otherwise, as exciting as it may be to date the lead singer, get ready to fight off some pretty creepy groupies.

## SAVIOR NEEDED?

He's at a local bookstore, browsing the biography section, when a very sexy woman gives him a quick smile. He notices, by the selection of books in her basket, her taste in literature is right up his alley. She smiles at him again and the tension between them seems to be building. Suddenly she drops one of her books and as she bends down to get it, he notices a tattoo of a tiger claw on her left breast.

He asks himself, "Did she just do that on *purpose?*"

She bends over again to place her basket on the floor, but this time she lifts her skirt slightly and yep, another tattoo above her knee, this time of a red dragon.

He can't help himself. "Nice tats."

She thanks him and they start chatting. After a few minutes, he asks her if she has time for a quick coffee. She does, and within about an hour over lattes, he finds out she is a single mother of two and she has an on-again, off-again addiction problem.

The guy in this situation has to ask himself if he keeps repeating the pattern of playing "the savior." Is he drawn to her *because* she's a single mom rather than her motherhood being incidental? Does he really like kids? Does he really like *her?* Was his mother a single mom? Is he perhaps trying to fix something from his past that he feels (unrightfully) responsible for?

The second issue here is the addiction. If this woman is an "on-again, off-again" addict, she might not quite be ready to be in a relationship and should instead focus on her own recovery and of course, the wellbeing of her children. This doesn't mean a person who has suffered with addiction can never have a good relationship. However, if your inclination is to "save," then this is certainly a red flag for *you.*

## FOOL ME ONCE, SHAME ON ME …
## FOOL ME TWICE, GET A THERAPIST

I have a buddy we'll call Oscar. Every time we've gone out – whether to a party, a bar or even a movie – he develops a monstrous crush on some woman. And no matter how many different females there have been for him to choose from, he seems to always fall for the one who treats him in the most appalling ways. I mean, these women are sadistic … even *cruel*. He's had women cheat on him, lie to him, call him names and even physically hit him and what does he do? He pines after them. The whole thing usually ends with her ridiculing his beautiful poetry attempts.

Oscar professes to hate this. He goes to psychoanalysis five times a week and is constantly talking about how all he really wants out of life is to find true love. He quotes from Shakespeare, Yates, even Shel Silverstein, and yet when it comes to his own life he just can't seem to, as he says, "meet the right girl."

But the deal is, he *can* meet the right girl; he just *chooses* the wrong ones. Somewhere along the way, he learned that being heartbroken is how love is. Maybe he subconsciously feels this pitiful position gets him attention, or that, somehow, being stepped upon and at some point let down is what defines him. Where did he learn this? Maybe this is a pattern he saw played out by one or both of his parents. Or perhaps this was the type of relationship he had with his first true love, and he's reliving the scenario either in order to fix it (which ultimately, of course, he can't do) or because it's all he knows.

We all know an "Oscar" (either a man or a woman), and many of us stand by, frustrated, as we watch our friend self-destruct. We don't want to see our friend treated badly, but isn't it easy to spot these bad decisions from the outside? When you're on the inside, all that love and lust and neuroses get jumbled up into one cloudy mess, and all clarity disappears. So calling them out can be tough – we're dealing with our *own* messed-up choosers and don't want to be the pot calling the kettle black.

## DAMSEL IN DISTRESS

Melinda would like to know the availability of Superman. Is he currently dating anyone? If not, how likely is it that he's on JDate? She prowls the Internet day and night in search of that man with the blue tights and X-ray vision. She knows her addiction to chaos will be cured if she can just find him. She gives herself permission to break down over every little thing, knowing her ego will one day be redeemed by the erstwhile Clark Kent. In other words, to quote Bonnie Tyler, she's "holding out for a hero."

The good news is there are tons of men out there willing to stand in for the role. The bad news is, Melinda mistakes the red flag waving so ferociously for a red cape, and then believes she is unable to function without her superhero. Her pattern is this: she falls apart, he steps in and puts her back together, she falls apart again. And so the cycle continues. She's Humpty Dumpty and he's "all the king's men," but if you remember the nursery rhyme, none of the king's horses or men could put Humpty together again.

Earlier we talked about the person who searches for someone to fix. Melinda exemplifies the person who searches for a fixer. You might suggest that those two types just call it day and get together, but this creates an unhealthy co-dependency and ultimately neither type will benefit.

If you find yourself always a choosing a fixer, ask yourself why you think you're so broken in the first place. You might be surprised that at the end of the day, you're able to save your own inner damsel, no matter how distressed.

## I AIN'T SAYING SHE'S A GOLD DIGGER

Before we even get started with this one, I have to attribute the above line to the great Kanye West. Yep, this is the same song I mentioned earlier as having cried to. Even now, as I just typed that line, I teared up a little. I don't understand it any more than you do. Okay, so I know a guy named Richard who is constantly saying things such as, "I just don't know where all my money goes." Once, he even declared this while at a Prada store buying a pair of chic sunglasses for his new girlfriend. "She just loves the bling," he'd said.

After scolding him for using the word "bling," I gently suggested to Richard that perhaps his hard-earned money was disappearing into his rela-

tionships. He ignored me while asking the saleslady if the 400-dollar pair of sunglasses had a matching necklace. You see, Richard attracts women who, for lack of a better description, value material items … highly … and subsequently value men who can *get* them said material items. I think you see where I'm heading here; Richard attracts gold diggers.

Here's how the red flags are disguised in his case: Richard thinks he just happens to favor women with good taste. What he fails to notice is that their good taste leads to massive spending on his dime. I suppose this would be fine if most of these women didn't break up with him after they've bled his credit cards dry, or as Billie Holiday said:

> *"Money, you've got lots of friends*
> *Crowding round the door*
> *When you're gone spending ends*
> *They don't come no more …"*

How can he spot these types of women? Well for one thing, if his girlfriend never makes the slightest attempt to pay for anything, this is a clue. Also, if a woman has a job that clearly can't possibly pay the rent and yet drapes herself in designer clothes, purses and cars, he should hear some alarms bells. Of course, she might have recently fallen on hard times or be a brilliant discount shopper, but it's worth noting. Another sign (and this one might be a tad more obvious) is if a date says something along the lines of, "Buy me a Mercedes or you'll get none of this," and then proceeds to squeeze one of her own fake breasts. You chuckle perhaps, but this really happened to Richard. And guess who has a brand new Mercedes?

If you're reading this and recognize yourself repeating the same relationships time and again, bear this in mind: Albert Einstein once said that the definition of insanity was doing the same thing over and over again and expecting different results. This is something we should all remember no matter what our particular pattern is. Recognizing the insanity is the first step in stopping it.

"Live by the harmless untruths that make you brave and kind and healthy and happy."

– Kurt Vonnegut

Here's a little "Cecily Fun-Fact:" When I was seven, I was asked by Randy Johnson's mother to "please stop calling her son 10 times a day after school." Yep, somehow between collecting glitter-stickers with my friends and doing homework, I found the time to endlessly call my second-grade crush, whom I referred to as "lover-boy." I think somewhere I even have a recording of me giggling uncontrollably while asking for said "lover-boy" in an English accent. (Incidentally, I learned that English accent from listening to Davy Jones. See how it all comes around full circle?)

Perhaps by now it's clear that I was boy crazy from a very early age. Actually, you could probably scratch the "boy" part out and surmise that I was just "crazy." Either way, I had (have) what some might call an unhealthy infatuation with the rougher gender. But the idea that I shouldn't make that known has always seemed strange to me. The notion that somehow it's wrong or unbecoming to call a boy (or show him any attention) freaks me out.

Here's what happened with lover-boy Randy: I did continue to call several times a day (not quite 10). To be honest, Randy never did seem super responsive. I believe the final straw was the day I popped his suspenders during reading comprehension class. He asked the teacher to tell me to "please stop

touching him." I still didn't get the hint, but eventually Randy and his family moved away. I don't want to believe they left town *because* of me, but I'm not gonna rule it out.

Here's another Cecily Fun-Fact: when I was in my 20s I once dated a guy who told me he was losing interest because he felt I was "too available." That's right, he said it right to my face, directly after I'd accepted another date with him. I was shocked and couldn't speak for a few seconds, so he continued: "I mean, I don't wanna be mean or anything, but I keep asking you out and you're, I don't know, making it too *easy* or something. You're always free." I thought about it and he was right; I *was* too free. So right then and there, I broke it off.✱

Since I was thinking this section would be about disproving the value of dating rules I guess these were not good illustrative examples, but I'd still like to explore these rules and put them to the test. Also, we'll take a look at other philosophies of dating.

I can tell you this right off the bat. One rule that seems to hold fast is the "don't pop people's suspenders" rule. You'd think I would have learned this lesson in second grade, but unfortunately I was reminded of it quite recently. Apparently this suspender-popping hurts, not unlike a popped bra, and as opposed to being seen as a form of flirtation, it might be inferred as an attack. (Why was the object of my desire wearing suspenders in the first place, you might ask? No, it wasn't Larry King, but I think it's best if you don't know the real answer.)

✱Okay remember when I said I broke it off with the guy who said I was "too available?" Sadly, that's a lie. I actually ended up continuing to accept dates (and sleeping) with him until he stopped calling. However, I wish I'd broken it off with him and if I could do it again … well …

## CHAPTER 5

# game. set. match?

Depending on how you look at it, I was either lucky or unlucky enough to be raised by an unconventional mom. Sure, she grew up in the '50s and had a few old-fashioned rules when it came to dating (one such rule was that if you're gonna trap somebody into getting you pregnant, make sure they're wealthy. I'm not entirely sure she was kidding); however, for the most part she believed in women doing whatever the hell they wanted in terms of courtship. If that meant calling a guy back or expressing true feelings through a letter, so be it.

I've clearly had no problem in the "calling a guy back" department. I've also poured my heart out more times than I can remember in letters to men and boys after whom I've lusted. There was the "you took a piece of my innocence" note to the poor guy I lost my virginity to. And of course the plethora of "why did you break my heart" letters to, well, the many guys who have broken my heart. (We'll visit that in a later chapter.)

The question is: what result was I expecting from pouring my heart out and did I achieve that result? I think with regard to the "break-up" letters, I was hoping to either change their minds or at least put it all out there so

I'd have no regrets. And while (so far) it has never changed anyone's mind, I honestly can say I don't regret being so transparent, despite what old-fashioned rule-setters might say.

Even though my mother was pretty liberated when it came to dating, she did stress the importance of playing your cards close to the vest. When I started to date, she'd often (almost incessantly) quote Neil Diamond's "Love on the Rocks" by reiterating, "When they know they have you, then they *really* have you." While logically this seemed like sound advice, I still struggled with the idea that love, lust, or even merely liking another person should be kept hidden. It took me years to figure out that there was a difference between letting my feelings be known and letting my feelings *control* me.

Friends, who I suppose were guided by their own mothers and grand-mothers, would often also advise me to back off in my pursuit of boys, as they claimed it might scare them off. "Let them come to you," they'd say. "You've gotta play the game." I recall I had a crush on a particular art student named Austin. After I asked him out, he told a mutual pal he'd "liked me, but was turned off because he didn't get to ask *me* out." He then proceeded to ask some guy named Donald to the prom, so once again my chooser was off.

Can I deny that there is some truth to this hard-to-get rule? I clearly cannot. I guess it does make sense that one should maintain a bit of mystery. This brings me to a series of books that began to come out in the mid-'90s, starting with *The Rules: Time-tested Secrets for Capturing the Heart of Mr. Right*, better known as just "The Rules." This book of guidelines, written by Ellen Fein and Sherrie Schneider, became a big hit and even developed a fe-

male prototype, later referred to as a "Rules Girl." Some of the ideas weren't especially new, but when I first read them I was flabbergasted. In addition to the fact that I felt it set the women's rights movement back a few decades, I thought, "How can these women lump men into one category? How can there be rules for love?" And yet some women adamantly insist that at least some of these tactics work, at least with regard to getting a man interested. (*Keeping* him interested is a different story.)

I'd like to put some of those rules to the test. Contrary to how it might seem, I have had a few somewhat successful long-term relationships. And yeah, most of them started out by my returning a few calls. I've put together a panel of three guys and three women, including me, and asked everyone to share their experiences with some of these rules. Here's a quick rundown of the panel:

**BETH:** 35-year-old single woman who had one broken marriage engagement. She describes herself as the ultimate "Rules" girl and, for the most part, follows them down to the very last word.

**DAVE:** 48-year-old divorced man. A straight shooter, he claims he doesn't believe in game playing, however seems to respond to those games. A self-admitted "man whore."

**JANE:** 25-year-old single woman. Loves the dating life, but is currently more focused on her pursuit of a career. Doesn't believe there are rules when it comes to life, let alone love. Believes in always going Dutch the first few dates and is a strong supporter of sexual liberation (and equality) for women.

**KENT:** 39-year-old single man. Extremely shy and confused when it comes to romantic love. Constantly reading self-help books with the hope of learning how to better approach women and sustain relationships.

| | |
|---|---|
| **JIM:** | 27-year-old engaged man. Has somewhat traditional beliefs when it comes to dating, although believes himself to be open to a more modern relationship. Met his fiancée on a skydiving trip with mutual friends. |
| **ME (CECILY):** | 30-something single woman. Attempting to search and explore every last relationship known to humankind, with the hope of figuring it all out. (Wish me luck!) |

So let's get started:

## RULE: KEEP THE STAR-69ING FOR THE BEDROOM

Let's begin with the "women should almost never call a guy and hardly ever call him back" rule. (I'm paraphrasing.) The actual guideline from the book is even more direct: "Don't call him and rarely return his calls." While I can't even imagine a world wherein women aren't supposed to call men they're interested in, apparently this one is popular among "Rules Girls." (And, incidentally, Randy Johnson's mother.) When asked, "What do you think about women initiating or returning men's calls during the courtship period?" this is how the panel responded:

| | |
|---|---|
| **JANE:** | When you say 'phone-calls,' does that also include texts? |
| **CECILY:** | In the first 'Rules' books this wasn't included, but let's assume in a more contemporary setting this means texts and instant messages as well as phone calls. |
| **JANE:** | That's the dumbest f%^#ing thing I've ever heard. |
| **CECILY:** | Why? |
| **JANE:** | Let me answer that with a question: Why would it be a |

good idea to begin a relationship with such an imbalance? If you're into someone, why pretend you aren't?

**BETH:** You're kidding, right?

**JANE:** Life is too short for unreturned calls. Put it this way: what if you meet a great guy and he calls, but you choose not to return it? After awhile, won't he just go away? Then you've missed out.

**DAVE:** Yeah, if a woman doesn't call me back after two tries, I write her off and assume she's not interested.

**BETH:** Sorry, but I find that hard to believe. If a guy really likes you, he's gonna keep trying whether you call him back or not. In fact, he'll like you more because you're a challenge. It sounds cliché, maybe, but it works.

**CECILY:** Jim, did your now fiancée ever call you back when you were dating?

**JIM:** Well yeah. I'm sure she did. Although she did play it cool the first six months.

**CECILY:** Explain, please.

**JIM:** If I remember right, I think she rejected me the first time I asked her out. After that, she said she had plans a lot and whether she did or not, I'll probably never know. The weekends she said she couldn't go out definitely made me think about her. I felt like I was pining for her a lot of the time.

**JANE:** I'm not saying that a woman should always make herself available. I just think it's kind of an extreme to say she should hardly ever return a call.

**BETH:** Think of it like this: do *you* like it when a guy is, like … fawning over you? Isn't it more exciting when you can't tell where he stands?

**JANE:** Not really, no. I like knowing where he stands.

**CECILY:** I have to admit, I've rarely had requited feelings for guys who were way into me. Kent, what do you think?

**KENT:** If I call a girl, which by the way takes me a good few weeks to summon the courage to do, and she's evasive or doesn't call me back, I shut down for weeks!

**JANE/BETH:** Awww!

**KENT:** I'm serious. I find this whole conversation unsettling.

**DAVE:** You need to get out more.

**KENT:** I know!

This "to call or not to call" debate then spiraled into a conversation about places Dave thought Kent might meet some serious "hotties" (his word, not mine). But a number of interesting perspectives appeared from this discussion. Some supported the rule while others absolutely did not.

## ARGUMENT IN SUPPORT OF THE PHONE-CALL RULE:

We just have to think back over the years to the guys and girls who made our and our friends' hearts flip. Were they the ones who were constantly batting their eyelashes or asking "how high" when we said "jump?" Nope. They usually kept us on our toes, wondering if they were interested. It would seem, based on this empirical data, that a woman not returning a man's call would aid in creating a sense of mystery and thus keep him interested for longer.

## ARGUMENT AGAINST THE PHONE-CALL RULE:

The risk women take by playing this coy hard-to-get game puts them in danger of losing out on a guy they might truly like. Some guys can't be bothered with such intense mind-f$%ks (like Dave) whereas others are far too shy and self-conscious to cope with confusing games, (like Kent). Either way, it's manipulative and risky, and I personally don't think it's worth it.

## CONSENSUS:

Based on the panel's reaction (and my own experience,) I'd stress the importance of finding a good balance between not being "too available" (as my Prince Charming accused me of) and not playing too many games. While we might not want to lay all of our cards on the table, I think it's far too extreme to "rarely return a phone call." By the way, Beth later admitted this hasn't always worked for her, however she stands by the fact that it makes *her* feel like she has more power.

And for the record, if *I* never called guys or returned their phone calls, I have no idea what I'd do with all that spare time. Really, that's seemingly all I do!

## RULE: MAKE HIM DO THE WORK

Another "rule" I find absurd is the insistence that a woman not meet a man halfway. This rule includes both meeting and paying for the date. Really? For serious? It's hard enough for me to imagine a dating universe where a woman isn't supposed to politely offer to pick up the tab now and then, let alone one where she's never supposed to even pay her own way. Who decided a woman's savings account is more important than a man's? Apparently, the "Rules Girls" have.

I believe that when two people are dating, if they make or have access to an equal amount of money, they should mostly split the tab. Sure, sometimes a man can be gallant and treat his companion to a lovely night on the town now and again. I admit I find this a generous and romantic gesture. That said, obviously a woman can treat the man too, and I'm sure it's as much appreciated.

However, if one of the two parties in a relationship is making bank and the other is struggling to pay the rent, then the person raking it in should probably treat most of the time. Isn't that just common sense? That goes not just for romantic relationships, but for close friendships as well. Sure you  have to be cautious you're not being used, but as long as that's not the case, why *not* treat your less-fortunate dates/friends?

As for never physically meeting a man halfway, well in my opinion that's just plain rude. Sure it's a nice gesture for a man to drive to a woman's side of town. So is it a nice gesture for her to head over to his side, or at least meet in the middle. But don't take it from me. Let's see what our panel has to say on these issues:

JIM: Well, I'm just gonna come right out and say it. I *do* think the guy should nearly always pay on dates. I guess I was just raised that way.

CECILY: So you actually think it's impolite to not pick up the tab?

JIM: On a date? Yeah, that's not polite.

KENT: But what if it's like the 10th date? You still have to pay?

JIM: I think, and correct me if I'm wrong, that a lot of women like to feel they're being taken care of. And I for one like to feel like I can provide.

JANE: I'm not gonna get all crazy on you and say it's a bad thing for you to want to treat us. I guess what I struggle with is the idea that we need to be provided for.

**DAVE:** You people are all crazy.

**JANE:** Who are you talking to?

**DAVE:** Mostly women. You're crazy. Half of you are saying you want us to pay for you and take care of things. Then the rest of you say you take offense to it.

**JANE:** Well I never said I took offense. I just don't want to feel like I'm dependent on anyone. If you want to pick up the tab to be chivalrous, great. But don't do it because you think I *need* it.

**DAVE:** That's what I'm talking about ... crazy. Although I'll give you this: if you make us always pay, we'll be broke and it will be tougher for us to cheat on you.

**JANE:** That's real nice.

**BETH:** If I could interject. I never offer to pay the tab. I mean maybe that's old fashioned, but I feel like it is a man's job to provide.

**JANE:** But then what's *your* job? To sit and look pretty?

**BETH:** It's just the nature of our genders.

**CECILY:** I don't understand that statement. What does that mean?

**BETH:** Just like what Jim said. Guys *like* to provide.

**DAVE:** Says *who*?

**CECILY:** Okay, well let me ask the guys this: how do you feel when a woman never offers to treat or go Dutch on dates?

JIM: I'm fine with it.

KENT: I don't think I am fine with that. I'm happy to treat the first few times, but after that, it's anyone's check.

DAVE: I maintain you're all nuts.

CECILY: Thank you, Dave. All right, let's look at the other part of that rule, which is for women not to meet men halfway.

DAVE: What does that even mean? That if I live on the west side of town and she lives on the east, I always have to go east?

CECILY: I think yeah, they mean men are supposed to make the effort.

DAVE: Screw that. Okay yes, I'll pick a woman up for a date. But once we start actually dating, she has to come get *me* some of the time. Not that I ever actually *date* anyone.

JIM: Why? I like driving over to my girlfriend's place.

KENT: Does it make you feel macho?

JIM: No, I just like it.

DAVE: It makes *me* feel like a douche-bag. Plus, my old girlfriend had cats and I hate cats.

CECILY: Let's not get off topic here. Beth, Jane, do you feel like you always want the guy to make it more convenient for you?

JANE: I think that sounds really selfish.

**BETH:** I've actually tried it. I never drove to my ex-fiancé's place, and if I spent the night there, he usually came and got me. He was fine with it. In fact, I think he felt like it helped him to put things on his terms. See, it's all about who feels like they have the power, whether they really do or not.

**JANE:** So what happened to your fiancé?

**BETH:** We broke up, but not because I wouldn't meet him halfway. We broke up because he cheated on me.

**DAVE:** He probably cheated on you with someone who would meet him halfway.

**BETH:** Cute.

## IN SUPPORT OF THE RULE TO MAKE THE GUY ALWAYS PAY:

I find it ridiculous, this idea that a woman should never go Dutch or pick up the tab. However, there are guys out there who want to feel like true providers and do not want their dates to pay. I would never want to discourage a man from treating a woman (or anyone else) in a generous manner and I'm pleased when the offer is made, but would hardly expect it.

## AGAINST THE RULE FOR THE GUY TO ALWAYS PAY:

A) How can women expect to be treated equally in, say, the workplace when they're always expecting the man to foot the bill?

B) While some men genuinely want to treat their girlfriends, lots of other guys think they should get a little sump'n sump'n in return. A friend of mine who lives in Israel said she feels she's expected to put out if she lets a guy pay, and she says her friends there feel the same. This doesn't mean all men (in any part of the world) think they deserve a little action in return for paying the check, but we can't dismiss this as something that *doesn't* happen. Or, as a friend once said when her date got irate that she wouldn't sleep with him after he had paid for their meal: "You asked me out for dinner. You didn't ask me out for dinner and a f#$%."

## IN SUPPORT OF THE RULE
## FOR WOMEN TO NEVER MEET HALFWAY:

Really? Some of us actually do this? This notion seems so trite and outdated it's hardly worth debate, but I don't even get the argument. Because it saves us on gas? Or maybe driving to his side of town makes us seem too available? Or if he drives, then the power balance shifts in his favor? Some self-proclaimed relationship gurus (I am not one of them) insist that when men maintain a gentlemanly attitude and make everything easier on their "kinder, gentler" female dates, the man retains more power … or at least the semblance of more power. For the record, Dave later refuted his own stance and agreed that women should never drive to the guy's place or even meet him halfway: "If you always pick her up, she'll never know where you live. That's gotta count for something, right?"

## AGAINST THE RULE FOR WOMEN
## TO NEVER MEET HALFWAY:

We're living in a modern age where – guess what? It's okay for women to drive. (I know … what a crazy idea!) This so-called rule, in the words of a friend of mine from high school, is "whack, yo" and in my opinion not worth any more discussion. (By the way, I went to high school a long time ago.)

## CONSENSUS:

We're not living in the 1950s. The soft, supple skin of a female will not crumble into perfumed dusting powder if she actually meets a guy on his side of town for lunch or picks up the tab. While Beth maintained she followed

this rule and got good results, she's still single, just like most of the panel. I
have lots of guy friends and have never once heard one say: "Ya know what I
like best about my girlfriend? She never reaches for the check and she always
makes me spend 30 minutes searching for a parking space at her apartment."
Yeah … despite the whole "less available" aspect, I'm calling bullshit on this one.

## RULE: DON'T STARE AT MEN OR TALK TOO MUCH

That's the exact rule listed in the book and I think the most hilarious one. In
fact, there's actually a suggestion that (and I'm paraphrasing) tells women
they should never make eye contact or smile at a man. Instead they should
just "smile at the room." No wonder guys think we're crazy. "La Ti Da, I'm not
making eye contact, I'm just smiling at this wall and now the floor and now
this chair. La La La, hope a guy notices how self-sufficient I am. I don't need
anything or anyone … except this bar stool … which I'm smiling at."

I think it's clear how I feel about this. But perhaps I'm talking too much
(which apparently I'm not allowed to do). Let me allow the panel to say a
few words:

**JANE:** Wait, so you're not supposed stare at men? What if
you're talking directly to him? Should you look at his
elbow?

**CECILY:** Dave, Kent, Jim – do you like it when a woman stares
at you?

**DAVE:** Like for how long? Like a creepy cat?

**CECILY:** No, just locking eyes.

**KENT:** I actually find it pretty hot. It obviously lets me know
they're interested.

**JIM:** Agreed.

**DAVE:** Depends on the girl. If it's Rosie O'Donnell, I don't really like it. If it's Grace Kelly, it's awesome.

**JIM:** Dude, how *old* are you? Is Grace Kelly even alive?

**DAVE:** You know what I meant. I'm just saying it's great if an attractive girl stares at you, but if she's not …

**JANE:** You're no Brad Pitt either.

**CECILY:** Anyway … so what would some of the arguments be in favor of the "women never staring at men" rule?

**JIM:** I guess some guys feel like if a woman looks at them too long, they're prey.

**JANE:** Oh, you mean like how women feel most of the time?

**JIM:** Yeah, but ya know … we're *supposed* to make you feel that way.

**CECILY:** We keep hearing that men traditionally have the hunting gene, but does this apply? Is a woman really "hunting" for a guy if she stares at someone she finds attractive? Isn't it just as obvious that she's into you if she goes out of her way to *not* look at you?

**JIM:** I think what you're all forgetting is that you can't group guys into just one category. Some are gonna be turned on by your looking at them and showing your cards and some aren't. We're not all the same, ya know?

**CECILY:** Good point, although we're trying to dissect these "Rules," so we have to kind of generalize. But yes, agreed … you're not all the same. So what do we think about women not "talking too much?"

**DAVE:**       I'm good with that rule.

**KENT:**       Me too.

**DAVE:**       I'm sorry to admit this but you ladies can be pretty chatty sometimes. My own mother, for example, will spend hours talking about people from her work that no one cares about.

**CECILY:**       Let's think about this in terms of dating. I think the rule is suggesting that women keep a lid on it, for the most part, on a date. Is this attractive to men?

**KENT:**       I actually like it when women do a lot of the talking, as long as the conversation is going both ways.

**JANE:**       Well, *obviously*! It doesn't matter if you're a man or woman … who'd want to just sit there and listen to another person yammer on about something?

**CECILY:**       Beth, you've been a follower of "The Rules." What does this mean to you?

**BETH:**       I don't know how literal this was meant to be. It doesn't mean a woman shouldn't be able to talk. It just goes back to that control thing again. Men don't want to feel dominated on dates.

**KENT:**       I do. I like to be dominated in nearly every aspect of my life.

**JANE:**       Kent, that's good to know. Beth, are you serious? Let's break this down: A) Do you really think if a woman talks "too much," whatever *that* means, she's somehow dominating a man? And B) Who cares if she is? I mean, what does any of this *mean*? There should be no rule or limit on how much a woman, or anyone for that matter, should be "allowed" to talk. This is all getting me so pissed off ...

**BETH:** Clearly. And that's not very attractive to men.

**DAVE:** Okay, Beth, now you're pissing *me* off. How can you say what's attractive or not attractive to all men? Oh and Jane? Pipe down.

**BETH:** All I'm saying is, from my understanding of this rule, men don't want to date their mothers. They don't need to hear about every aspect of your day. That's what your female friends are for.

**JANE:** Right, wouldn't they want to date their equals? And please tell me why it's unattractive to men that I'd get angry at the idea of being submissive?

**BETH:** It's unattractive to everyone to be angry.

**CECILY:** But why should women resign themselves to the idea of having to be submissive?

**BETH:** Well, I thought we were talking about what works in the dating world. Letting a guy be dominant works.

**CECILY:** Based on this panel, that just isn't true for everyone.

This conversation went on for quite some time and seemed to continuously come back to the idea of dominance and submission in the dating world. With the exception of Beth, the panel (including me) was pretty adamant against the notion that women should put a sock in it or curb their desire to look at a man for too long. (Granted, it should be noted that regardless of gender, *no one* should stare at *anyone* for, say, two hours. That would be creepy.)

## IN SUPPORT OF THE
## "NO STARING OR TALKING TOO MUCH" RULE:

I can't think of any. Except well, maybe … nope, still nothing. However, Beth maintains her belief that women should let the man take control on dates. She says this doesn't leave women without a voice; it just manipulates men into believing they have the power. (FYI, "manipulates" was her choice of words and, I have to say, a very good one.) Dave also went on to say he can feel super freaked out if a woman stares at him because it makes him wonder, "did I give her the clap and just don't remember?"

## AGAINST THE
## "NO STARING OR TALKING TOO MUCH" RULE:

I find this suggestion (ahem, sorry, "rule") to be utterly absurd and offensive. What was even *more* offensive was Dave, who later said (and I hope he was joking), "If a woman stares at me really intensely, it's tougher for me to slip something into her drink." Could *this* be what "The Rules" women had in mind? I doubt it.

It's fair to say, as Jane pointed out, that *no one* should speak too much without also listening, but other than that basic principle of conversation etiquette, this idea is just silly. I'll leave it at that.

## CONSENSUS:

Women who conceal their thoughts and feelings (by not allowing themselves to show interest or speak freely) are not only doing a huge disservice to the state of equality, they are hiding who they really are. Even if it's true that some men are attracted to women who play hard to get (and I'm not sure it is), then these women are attracting them on false pretenses.

Manipulative game playing at such a high level is both outdated and dangerous. You might not want to show all of your cards – this is true at the beginning of *any* new venture. But to worry about how long you're looking at someone is to dissect romance into such tiny pieces that it becomes unrecognizable. Probably goes without saying, but my vote on this one is "nay."

Although a few of "The Rules" make sense to me, such as "Don't rush into sex" and "Don't date a married man" (ya think?) I find most of them hilariously ridiculous. Such suggestions as "Let him take the lead," and my personal favorite, "Don't discuss 'The Rules' with your therapist" illustrate just how painfully old fashioned these rules are. That last one suggests an abusive relationship with the writers of *The Rules*: "Shush, baby … there's no need to tell anyone about this. Remember, these rules are just between us … got it?" Wouldn't you think it was odd if I told you to heed my advice and then advised you to not share said advice? Yeah, something's rotten in the state of feminism.

Then there are the guy's manuals. I know a bartender we'll call Mark who used to come over late at night (hey, I was 22) and insult my furniture. The more he'd do it, the more confused I'd get about his feelings for me and, more interestingly, *my* feelings for *him*. It seemed so odd to have a man who clearly wanted to get in my pants show such mixed signals. And it wasn't that I was so sensitive about my futon; it was that his disrespect and backhanded humor seemed so contrived. I couldn't figure it out. (I also continued to make out with him – *not* because he was a dick, but because he was a great kisser. There, I said it.)

It wasn't until a few years later that I realized he was doing this on purpose. A mutual friend later told me Mark had followed one of the many guidebooks written specifically for men. Eventually Mark admitted this to be true, although he never would tell me which one. Based on my research, I'm gonna guess it was *The Game: Penetrating the Secret Society of Pick-Up Artists*, written by Neil Strauss, or something along those lines.

Although at times *The Game* can give colorful advice on the art of picking up women, some of its counsel is pretty mean. And yep, Strauss definitely taps into a concept called "negging," which is to basically insult your date or figuratively knock them (in a light, playful way) into submission. On a more positive note, Mark's "negging" inspired me to trade in the nasty futon I'd found on the side of the road for a proper couch. Thanks Mark!

There is certainly nothing wrong with digging into different philosophies to try and find out what makes the opposite sex tick. I mean, that *is* what we're doing *here,* after all. My issue is when it becomes a manifesto. "Do *this* and men will marry you … do *this* and women will sleep with you." The belief that we're all robots in search of marriage or sex (depending upon our gender) is insulting, and the idea that one person or book can tell us all how to accomplish these goals is even more so.

I think it's safe to say that most of these "Rules" are irrelevant, if not downright disturbing. There's really only *one* rule we need to live by (besides always wearing protection) and I will lay it down for you now. (I personally think it's more valuable than any of the others we've discussed.) Ready? *Don't email ex-boyfriends (or anyone) once your Ambien (or the like) has kicked in.* How might you *know* it has kicked in? If you're watching TV and that 1-800-closet organizer commercial comes on, ask yourself if you feel pure joy upon seeing that little dancing stick figure. If you *do* feel pure joy, it has kicked in. Step away from the computer (or BlackBerry) and go to sleep. Trust me on this one.

Oh, by the way, here's a quick update on our panel:

**BETH:** Met a guy recently with whom she claims she practices most of the "Rules." She admits she's a bit confused, however, because her ex-fiancé recently also came back into the picture. She says she's trying to "play it cool" with both men and see how it unfolds.

**DAVE:** Still very, *very* single although insists he's getting laid a lot. Doesn't actively practice any gaming techniques, but admits that acting "aloof and asshole-ish" comes naturally.

**JANE:** Got a new job in the entertainment field and met a man she describes as a sensitive metrosexual. Still maintains that she finds game playing "repulsive" and says she "refuses to be anyone other than 'herself.'"

**KENT:** Has read literally 15 self-help books in the last six months. Still refers to himself as "extremely shy," although recently joined an online dating site, which has helped him gain confidence. Is still, as he puts it, "searching for answers."

**JIM:** Now happily married. He thinks some pick-up advice is helpful, even though he claims "he's never really needed it."

**CECILY:** Has ultimately no idea. Does, however, have a lot more stories to share. So let's get going ...

> "How bold one gets when one is sure of being loved."
>
> – Sigmund Freud

I dated a guy a few years ago we'll call "Miguel." After just a dash of playing-hard-to-get tactics (Oh, who am I kidding? I made out with him the first night I met him.) I enjoyed a brief courtship with him, which ended with my referring to him as a "lying dumb-ass" and him making reference to *me* as a "psycho-slut." But before we relive that lovely storybook ending, let's take a look at how we got there:

Miguel was charming, with frat-boy dimples, perfect teeth and a weird young-Mickey Rourke mystique. In fact our whole four-month encounter was reminiscent of the film *9½ Weeks*, except without most of the sex stuff. Oh, and it was 16 weeks. Now that I think about it, the only *9½ Weeks* quality about it was one time I ate a hot pepper in front of him at dinner.

I should mention that from the get-go, Miguel and I were ill suited. Remember that whole chapter about "fixing our choosers" and spotting the flags? Yeah, well I wish I'd had *me* around to teach me that back then. Without revealing too much, let's just say Miguel was an "officey-office" type person. He was the head of human resources at a cell phone company. And it's not that I had a problem with him working in an office (because there's certainly nothing wrong with that). No, I took issue with the fact that he personified the office culture, like a stereotype. He loved living the office life. He'd joke by saying things like: "Don't talk to me till I've had my coffee." Better yet, that (hilarious) line would be written on his coffee mug, so he wouldn't *have* to say it. He was the "TGIF" guy who shows up at Houston's to hang out with the HR girls after a "grueling" day to do impressions of his boss while drinking something called "The Tornado." He's the guy who scowls at you for asking to order more paper clips and then says, "Just kidding … how many d'ya need?"

When we began our little relationship, I thought my late nights and unconventional work ethic were impressive to him. It turns out that on the contrary, he was appalled that I didn't work out or that I *occasionally* slept in my clothes. He never could grasp the fact that I always asked for an extra shot of Patron in my margaritas and I could never grasp the fact that he yammered on so much about his 401K plan. (Actually, had he not been such a Chatty Cathy, perhaps I wouldn't have *had* to ask for extra Patron.)

Mind you, this wasn't your average "Oscar/Felix" dichotomy. I mean as far as I know, Oscar and Felix never made out in the back seat of Felix's Mustang. This thing we had was different in the sense that we had some *serious* chemistry going on. The problem seemed to be that in the end, the chemistry didn't make for an exciting explosion. Instead we were left with just a tiny scrap of sulfur. But let's not get ahead of ourselves.

All right, I'm gonna admit it right now. I did get a little crazy at the end (although never slutty, so the term "psycho-slut" was inappropriate). After dating just shy of four months, Miguel called me and said the following: "You're a lot of fun, Cecily. A *lot … of … fun.*" (He literally said it like that, punching every word for effect.) "But I've given this some thought and I've decided that you're the kind of girl you just have fun with. You're not like, ya know, a long-timer."

Now since this isn't the chapter on break-ups, I'll refrain from revealing too much of the aftermath, but I will say there was some crying. This was not a result of my believing Miguel to be "the one," but rather the fact that anyone would have the balls to say something like that. I'm pretty sure I hurled a few insults at him like "Hey, well, the only real package in your life is the *severance* packages you give out at work," (which I guess was supposed to be some kind of small penis reference) and "Here's a recommendation letter: F#$% You." Tacky stuff like that.

After a few exit-interview emails, I finally got out of him that he'd met someone else and had been two-timing me for the last month of the relationship. (I guess apparently it was someone who could be a "long-timer.") Luckily for both of us, it all ended before I could nurture my inner crazy to unknown heights and he could lie beyond repair. But I often ask myself just what made us both so unable to contain our worst sides? And why, when we both knew the other was wrong for us, did we continue to date?

The following chapter isn't just about relationships gone wrong; it's about the good ones too. But it still asks the question: can differing perspectives between genders render even relationships with promise impossible? If we can pinpoint the little nuances that make men and women drive each other crazy, could we avoid them?

# CHAPTER 6

# And ... We're Off!

Aw, the Honeymoon Period. Surely you know of what I speak: the sweet beginning of most relationships where all our crazy bullshit (or most, anyway) is tucked away, hidden from the sightlines of our new lovers. It is that lovely time when new couples bask in the glow of discovery. Everything is new and no one is needy, because we (well, most of us) haven't developed attachments yet. Once we do, watch out.

Let's say you've waded past the game playing and manipulative rule-abiding courtship and find yourself in a real grown-up exclusive relationship. Perhaps until this point you've refrained from revealing to your new companion those little quirks, like you still sleep with your favorite stuffed animal or you occasionally bang your ex. You get the idea ... you're not completely *you*.

This is common and, in fact, probably a good idea. Just as we ease into a steaming hot bath, we have to ease into the process of getting to know each other. I think this is how we ultimately get hooked. Everything starts out so nicely that our minds (and bodies) keep craving that first hit, even once things turn sour.

For the most part, we all initially put our best faces forward, even in the healthiest of relationships. On a personal note, I know it takes me *at least* four months before I let guys know I'm still obsessed with Duran Duran. Sure I could make that known on a first date, but lots of men are intimidated by Simon LeBon's abs. What were we talking about? Oh yeah … the trick is to surf the line between easing into a relationship and withholding information. And sometimes that line can be very hard to navigate.

"Withholding" is a word that has been thrown around a lot in recent years. It can be used as a verb or an adjective, as in "You are withholding

your feelings," or "That guy is a withholding person. Also, he's an ass."
(Just had to throw in that last line to keep it realistic.) You can either be
withholding with literal information or with your feelings, but either way you
choose not to share details about yourself that are significant in your connection with another person. Basically, withholders lie by omission.

Aside from the rare folks who wear their hearts (and pasts) on their
sleeves, most of us withhold at least a little. But how do we decide what to
reveal early on and what to hold back? Here's where I differ from most relationship advisors. I'm a firm believer that, while we don't have to spill all of
our crazy on the first few dates, we should treat our romantic companions
the same as we do our best friends (especially if you *sleep* with your best
friend). I think as long as we keep working on our own self-actualization
(i.e., we know and understand who *we* are) we should be able to share that
with our lovers.

Think about how open you are with your best friends. Why should
the person you're dating receive any less of you than the people you pal
around with? Okay, so maybe you can refrain from talking about your teeth
whitener or highlights, but at the end of the day, shouldn't that man *be*
your best friend?

"But," you may ask, "does being really open with someone mean your
sex life with them has to suffer?" No. Honestly, I believe the best relationships stem from the closest of friendships and, in fact, the *more* of you that
gets let out, the more vulnerable you are and the better the sex!

For me, a long time was wasted on believing I could have hot, passion-
ate sex only with guys that were wrong for me (see Chapter Four). While,
yeah, okay, I still struggle with that a little, I have learned through trial and
error that my best relationships were with guys with whom I could really
be myself.

With one guy who comes to mind (we'll call him Henry) I was able to let
down all my guards. I was *me*, without withholding emotions, memories or
information, and subsequently it was a very deep love. When we open up
like this we do risk putting our neuroses on display, and sometimes that can
be tough to swallow. That is what happened with Henry and ultimately he
dumped me for a gynecologist. (Really, speaking of "on display!") However,
having experienced this type of deep relationship, I still truly believe it was
worth the risk.

Let's look at some examples of how to let yourself out slowly. Let's say you've been dating your companion for a few months and you want your true self to shine. You *want* to tell your boyfriend or girlfriend that you're addicted to really sleazy reality television, but you're afraid he or she will judge you. Do you say A) "Honey, I can't go out tonight because I have to watch 14 back-to-back episodes of *America's Next Top Model*," B) "I have no more use for you, as I've decided to marry my TiVo," or C) "Hey, what TV shows do you watch?"

If you're anything like me (or exactly like me) you answered both A and B. Sadly I had to learn the hard way that this was probably not the best move. The truth is, had I gone with C, I wouldn't have been withholding, but rather just timidly testing the waters. I'd have been discovering him while slowly letting him know me.

Let's try another one. Say, you're a month or two in and need to tell your companion that your landlord also happens to be your ex. (Now *this* is a nice setting for a porno.) Perhaps you and said landlord had dated for quite some time and had even gotten serious at one point, but things ended amicably and you both moved on. Your new lover has *met* the landlord, but doesn't know about your past. Do you: A) Say "Remember how I told you I had a leaky bathtub? Yeah, well my landlord used to caulk it ... and me." B) Say "Listen, now that we're getting more serious, I need to tell you that I used to date my apartment manager, but it's obviously over and we have no other feelings than friendship. Are you cool with that?" or C) Try to make your companion think they're crazy by insisting you told them on the first date, e.g., "So, remember how I used to bang Jim/Jean. That was funny, right?"

It should be relatively clear that the best solution here is B, although A and C might make for a good laugh. (For the record, this is one of the few things that did not actually happen to me, but the situation did occur with one of my friends.) Although it might initially be a tough conversation, it's best to be up front and clear. The longer you wait, the harder it will be to reveal the truth and the more you will appear to have been withholding. Plus, as we discussed, you're building a friendship as the basis for your new relationship, and honesty and trust must be part of that foundation for it to hold strong. If the relationship is healthy, something like this shouldn't be an issue, as long as you assure your companion there's nothing to worry about.

## STATIC CLING?

So you've made it past the Honeymoon Stage and are in a full-swing day-to-day relationship. You're seeing each other's bits and pieces, both physically and emotionally. Hopefully at this point you've got both feet in (or at least a foot and a half). This is when it goes from "exciting and new" to "could this be a good match?" And this is also when those patterns we keep repeating come into play. We all have them, those *things* we do with mate after mate after mate. We don't even know we're doing it half the time, and if we are aware, we don't know how to change it. All we do know is that this pattern almost always leads to a not-so-positive result.

I'll start by telling you my pattern. With most relationships, I start out in what I *think* is a power position. For a long time I thought it was attractive to act as though I was so independent I didn't need much from anyone. Usually, I'd go on and on about how we women "need to maintain our sense of self" and how we "came into this world alone, we're going out the same way, blah ... blah ... blah." While I'm still not a huge fan of people who lose their "I"s

and become "We"s, (especially the ones who are constantly saying stuff like; "*We* love the band Oasis and *we're* pregnant," and "*We* don't like the fact that you look like you hate us, Cecily.") I realize it's okay to show up front that you're willing to be cared for.

Here's where I really go wrong. The whole, "I'm independent, with no needs from you" thing is bullshit. I *do* have needs, and by not relaying that at the start, I'm setting a precedent that my new companion has no reason to question. Then when my truer self begins to show, I appear needier than I would have had I not made such a fuss about it. Usually at this point the guy begins to withdraw. (Read: "I'm not dealing with this psycho clingy crap.") The more he withdraws, the more I cling, and round and round we go until the whole thing collapses in on itself like a giant dying star. (Dramatic, perhaps, but I'm making a point.)

The thing is I can now see this pattern, which is a good start. And I know it doesn't make me a terrible person, nor is the guy who responds this way necessarily a d-bag. But it does illustrate one of the many push-pull routines women and men are likely to get into, contributing to the "she's crazy, he lies" factoid. Ya see, he thinks *she's* nutso because she gets clingy and maybe even emotional, and *he* might tell a fib or two to avoid the drama.

Women can also be the avoiders and men can be extremely clingy (I've witnessed this firsthand). But whichever way it falls, we have to be aware of these cycles if we have any hope of breaking them. What's that thing *you* do? Do you find yourself clinging while your companion pulls away? Or do you find yourself spinning such a complicated, silky web of lies that you get trapped? This brings us to the other main point of all this...

## "LIES, LIES, LIES...YEAH"

How many times have you heard this one: "Baby, I *had* to lie to you ... you're so sensitive" or: "Sweet-ass, it's just a little fib. You'd have killed me if you knew the whole truth." And how many times have you gotten furious and insisted that you'd rather hear the *truth*, despite it sometimes being ugly, than be lied to? Well guess what ... *that* is a lie. Or at least it might be, depending on the circumstances.

Now before you get all up in my grill, (why have I suddenly started talking like that) let's think about this for a minute. Please turn your attention to exhibit A, that old cliché relationship question, "Do these jeans make me look fat?" Most women (and even quite a few men) at one time or another have asked this, hoping the answer will be a resounding "No." And yet even though we ask, most of us are not prepared for the pure truth, even if it's something benign, such as: "Those jeans make you look how you look."

You see, most of us want to hear, "No, those jeans make you look fabu-lous." Because at that very moment, although we can't change the size of our ass, we *can* convince ourselves that it looks good. But we think we can't do it without your approval, which is why we ask that very loaded question. Now before I proceed, I should point out that I am aware there are people who are willing to hear the truth and whose egos don't need white lies. But (and I speak for myself as well) many of us operate with thinner skin.

Let's move on to a less-clichéd example and pose the following question of our mate: "Who did you have lunch with at work today?" Maybe the *truthful* answer is, "Jimmy, John and Tatiana, that new 22-year-old D-cupped intern." And let's say the *revised* answer is, "Oh, Jimmy and John." Is that a lie? Well,

technically no, because Jimmy and John *were there*. But is it the whole truth? You bet your ass (which incidentally looks great in those jeans) it isn't.

Now this one is a bit fuzzier. The lie-by-omission tactic isn't the same as an innocent white lie. A white lie is, by definition, a lie committed in order to make someone feel good. "You always look perfect in those jeans" is a lie meant to make the wearer of said jeans feel good (or at least better) about herself. The "I forgot to mention the 22-year-old D-cupped intern I had lunch with" lie is to protect the person who omitted it. See how that changes things a wee bit?

Here's where things can really get cloudy. Remember in Chapter Two when we talked about men and women being biochemically wired differently? Apparently women are more adept at reading social cues, ticks and yes, sometimes even lies. (It's important to mention that although the term "women's intuition" has been around for years, we may not always interpret data correctly. This can lead to false accusations, which could earn us a crazy status.) That aside, we can often pick up on those little nuances that alert us when something is just a tiny bit off.

So back to the point; when the guy leaves out the intern's name, there might be a signal indicating the omission, e.g. "I had lunch with Jimmy and John and this ... oh, yeah, that's it." Or they'll do that thing where they buy time by repeating the question (and this, if you would like a lesson in sleuthing, is one of the top ways cops figure out you're lying): "Who did I have lunch with? Who? Oh yeah, just Jimmy and John." My personal favorite is the "truth, sniff, lie" tactic, which goes a little something like this: "I had lunch with Jimmy and John, "sniff" and ... that's about it." I'm not sure what it is exactly about the sniff that makes people (read: men) do it when they're fibbing, but if I figure it out I'll let you know.

Is it okay for either men or women to lie, especially when it's only serving their needs? No. But do we understand why it's done? Sure. By that same token, is it okay for women or men to lose their minds and accuse each other of everything? Of course not. But once we get ourselves all wrapped up in the drama, it's hard for either side to refrain. Drama is an important word to focus on here, because if we stop to think about relationships, that's what all that the clinging, accusing and lying comes down to: drama. We, each of us, can attempt to stop the cycle by merely following a few simple rules:

1  **Don't continually ask rhetorical questions for which you have already written the answer**, e.g. "Am I pretty?" "Does this outfit make me look huge?" "Do you honestly think that stripper is hot?" Insecurity is not an attractive attribute, and while there's nothing wrong with wanting some reinforcements now and again, you don't want to appear like you *need* them incessantly. (Also, for the record, strippers are often hot, albeit in a sleazy way, so it's best not to ask if you don't want the answer.) However, if you *never* receive compliments from your companion, you have the right to be bummed. Personally, I think lovers should shower each other with kind words, so it's certainly okay to discuss the issue if you feel neglected. Just try not to do it in a leading, passive-aggressive way.

2  **Tell the truth more often than not.** If your companion asks if a certain pair of pants make her behind look large, it's okay to say something like "Those are okay, but the grey pants are even better." However, if changing is not an option (i.e., you're already in the car en route to a party), there's nothing wrong with giving your friend the support he/she needs.

**3** This might go without saying, but I'm gonna say it anyway: **It's a good idea not to engage in activities about which you'll later feel compelled to lie.** In other words, if you don't want to have to tell your girlfriend that you had lunch with a hooker, don't have lunch with a hooker. Each relationship will have its own set of boundaries, and things will always pop up to test your relationship and those boundaries. It's an ongoing process, so it's important to keep communication alive. But I'm pretty sure "lunch" with a hooker would cross the boundary in most relationships.

**4** **If you find yourself getting angry or scared or jealous, remember these are normal emotions.** The key is to not react to them immediately, as usually a little perspective is helpful. So, for example, if you tend to have a jealously problem and see your mate flirting at a dinner party, go in the other room, take a deep breath and count to 20. Then you can let the more logical part of your frontal lobe determine the best solution. Nine times out of 10, I think you'll find that screaming and accusing won't be it. (Although I do find throwing stuff, say a flower vase, is a good rational choice. I jest.)

**5** **Hold on to your core being and let your companion do the same.** Men and women will both withhold (there's that word again) parts of themselves they believe won't be desirable to their mates. Ultimately, they'll wind up resenting their partners because they feel they aren't shining as brightly as they once did. The truth is we have no one to blame but ourselves for this. If you refrain from attempting to control your mate in addition to yourself, hopefully you will grow *together*. You will have to make compromises along the way, but never compromise the core of who you are for someone else. (Unless "who you are" is a serial killer or jewel thief. Then it might be okay to compromise your core.) Sure we all have room to change and learn and grow. But we have to make sure we're doing it for healthy reasons and not out of fear or jealousy or neediness.

So in summary, try not to be crazy and try not to lie. I guess I could have just *said* that. With all this talk about compromises and taking deep breaths and growing, you probably thought I forgot about one of the most important relationship elements: *sex*! Put your fears to rest because in the next chapter, we're gonna take *this* relationship to a whole new level …

"It started out with a kiss, how did it end up like this?"

– The Killers

My first time involved a Bruce Springsteen record, a small town in New Jersey and a hot summer day. I remember it clearly, except for some reason I can't picture the guy's face (and I'd dated him for over six months), but then again this was a few years back. Yeah, I waited till I was nearly 21 to lose my virginity – not so much because I thought it was precious, but more because I was scared out of my mind (and eventually out of my pants).

What I also do remember is that it was awful. I say this not as a dig at the poor, very sweet guy, but as a comment on my expectations. In the movies, there are violins playing (or at least a cheesy Green Day song), doves flying around and/or waves gently lapping in as the first-time lovers embrace. Even on, say, *The O.C.*, sweet music underscores the intensity between virgins, as they longingly stare at one another, completely in the moment, and gently kiss each other's pouting lower lip, bathed in a candlelit glow.

I don't know what moment I was in, but this was not my experience. There were no doves or violins, but I *do* remember the AC finally popped itself on just when the heat had become unbearable, so at least there was that. I also remember that it didn't last even as long as a Green Day song, but for that I

was thankful. In fact, the whole thing couldn't have taken longer than three minutes, which was not even enough time for Bruce to finish wailing about where he was born (turns out it was the U.S.A.).

Oh it gets better. After this very important awkward union, my "boyfriend" at the time (whose fraternity nickname, by the way, was "Slug") shuffled off to play video games. I, on the other hand, locked myself in the bathroom and proceeded to write Slug a very long, heartfelt letter about how he'd "taken a piece of my childhood." It went on and on about innocence lost and "flowers blooming" and blah, blah, blah. I swear, I think I even quoted an Indigo Girls song. Oh my.

POOR SLUG! The look on his face when he read that letter was that of utter fear. I mean c'mon … what 20-year-old guy wants to read a poem about sex written by lesbian folksingers? I'll tell you this much, Slug didn't. But he patted me on the head and said something like: "Thanks, buddy," and this silently confirmed what I already knew … he wasn't the one.

Slug and I broke up shortly after that magical east coast day, but my experience with sex – well thankfully that got a whole lot better, although it took me some time to get there. Because I'd gotten such a slow start, the concept took awhile to unfold from something foreign and scary to something wonderful. I had to learn to trust my body and try new things. (I also had to learn to insist that Bruce Springsteen songs be kept to a minimum in the bedroom.)

It's amazing how much the topic of sex comes up in our lives. People are either scared of it, obsessed with it or constantly in search of it. And yet many folks can't even seem to get a handle on a good kiss. But what's even more amazing to me is the different way we genders seem to attach meaning to sex. Is it a challenge, a stress-reliever, a contract, a life alteration? The response really depends on who's telling the story. And so now, without further ado, let us take a look at sex from a few different angles.

## CHAPTER 7

# Tales from the Bed

Let's begin this chapter with the sex talk I had with my mother when I was four. I'd asked her the big question, "Where do babies come from?" I remember the day well and that I had needed this information not because I was feeling especially maternal or even inquisitive, but because I wanted to return my doll to wherever it was that babies came from, and therefore needed to know.

I remember feeling at the time that I'd made my mom uncomfortable. She stared at her velvet painting of Elvis for a moment and then said, "Well, dear ... where do you *think* babies come from?" I took this question very seriously. *Hmm, where did I think babies came from?*

"Well ... when a rooster-bird sits on a lady's stomach, he lays a rooster egg," I'd said, hopeful.

"Yes? Go on."

"And then the rooster egg hatches on the lady's stomach and then crawls inside the belly button. That is what makes a baby. And all people are birds before they're people."

My mom was quiet for another beat and then said, "That is honestly *exactly* what happens. Rooster eggs. Well done." She didn't have the heart to tell me every facet of my theory had been wrong. Roosters don't lay eggs at all, let alone on the stomachs of women. And how would a bird-baby crawl inside a belly button? It couldn't. But this is what I believed and would continue to believe until I happened upon the movie *Porky's* on cable TV years later.

Speaking of *Porky's*, what that early '80s raunch-comedy taught us about sex is both priceless and almost as wrong as my initial rooster theory. Of course, then there was the movie *Hardbodies*, which for me raised the question: "Why even bother having a plot when the *name* of your movie is '*Hardbodies*'?" That led to *Fast Times at Ridgemont High*, the movie that inspired my friend Gretchen to use a carrot when teaching me the finer art of you-know-whats. And let's not forget the aforementioned *Porky's*, which opened our young impressionable minds to all kinds of notions about what sex really was.

The first misguided theory *Porky's* put in my head was the idea that within every group of friends there would be a bad-boy, a nerd, an athlete and a hick, and although they were all different, they'd stick together through thick and thin. (Granted, John Hughes released *The Breakfast Club* a few years later based on nearly the same formula, but his version didn't involve the hiring of prostitutes.)

The second misconception I can attribute to this film was that boys might try to lose their virginity through random peepholes in the ladies' locker-room wall. After seeing the infamous locker-room scene (which at the time truly terrified me), I vowed to never be naked in a locker room. If I'd

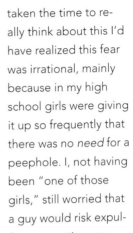

taken the time to really think about this I'd have realized this fear was irrational, mainly because in my high school girls were giving it up so frequently that there was no *need* for a peephole. I, not having been "one of those girls," still worried that a guy would risk expulsion to deface school property in the hopes of glimpsing me putting on a pair of Doc Martens.

What *Porky's* (and many other movies of its ilk) got *right* was the fact that most people, both men and women, want to get laid and there always has to be a first time. The expedition from virgin to non-virgin is an exciting albeit scary one, and for some (including me) it doesn't always go as it was planned in our heads (or by '80s comedy directors).

## THE FIRST-TIMERS CLUB

Here are two stories from folks who asked me to use fake names (wimps). They illustrate that it doesn't matter if you're a man or a woman; the first time for either can be tragically unpredictable.

## JOHN'S FIRST

After waiting until his mid-20s for the big day, John decided to lose his virginity to a stranger he met in a bar. The fact that she spoke only broken English didn't seem to deter him and in fact actually turned him on. After a mere two hours of being bought drinks, she (we'll call her Martina) pointed toward his car and gave him the international sign for "blow-job." (And you thought Slug was romantic.)

They went to John's house. After they had been fooling around for a few hours, she asked him, and I quote, to "please make her a condom." He, being a bit confused, wanted to confirm that she indeed wanted to have sex, so he pulled out a Trojan from the bedside and asked, "You want me to put this on?" She nodded and again said gleefully, "please to make the condom."

So John "made the condom," but as they began to have sex, Martina got just a little bit emotional. John, nervous as he already was, noticed a tear running down her cheek and of course stopped immediately. "Are you okay, Martina?" he asked.

"John," she replied, "I have thousands of feelings for you and my feelings spill from my eyes. Please to make another condom."

"What?" he understandably asked. She repeated herself, and while many men might at this point say something like "I think we should just lie here a bit and hang out," John "made another condom" and started up again. And again, Martina began to cry. John stopped and said, "Okay, something is clearly wrong here. I don't think we should do this."

"John," Martina said, wiping her wet eyes. "In Panama, girls who make tears during making of love are girls made of angels. Please, PLEASE to make one more condom."

"I don't know what you're saying. But okay." Yep, okay indeed as once again, John reached for a third condom. Wanna guess what happened next? Yes that's right, after beginning a third bout of sex with Martina, she began to cry once more, only this time it was a lot louder. John sadly had to abort his mission, as he was unable to complete it. (Which was not surprising, considering it was his first time.)

Just for the record, Martina immediately put her clothes on and called a taxi to take her home (or back to the bar or wherever she went). John stopped going to the pub in which he met her and never saw her again. He does, however, still think of her fondly anytime he passes a box of Trojans in the grocery store. Or a box of tissues.

Is there a lesson to learn from this story? If a woman (or man for that matter) begins to cry during sex, do *not* continue no matter how much she/he begs. Trust me, people; it's not worth it. (Note: if you're still able to perform while your lover is crying, proceed directly to the nearest therapist's office and have yourself checked in for sensitivity training.)

## AMY'S FIRST

Amy, like John, got a late start with her sex life. And also like John, she met her first-time lover in a bar after drinking copious amounts of booze. (Wouldn't it have been great if she'd just met *John* in that bar? But it wasn't John, it was a guy we'll call Roger.) Because this was her neighborhood pub and he worked there, she'd actually known him for quite some time.

Roger and Amy barely noticed when the lights came up at 2:00 am. They'd been making out in one of the back booths (damn tequila!) and things were getting pretty hot and heavy. Amy decided she'd waited long enough for Prince Charming and was just gonna have to settle for a guy who perhaps owned a Prince record. Close enough, right?

After inviting Roger back to her place, it didn't take long for either of them to shed their clothes and get down to it. But things suddenly got confusing when, sadly, Roger stopped and sat up.

"What's wrong?" Amy asked.

Roger was blushing. "I ... I ... had a little accident."

"What happened?"

"Well, I got so excited by the idea that you're a virgin, I kinda had a premature situation."

Amy, despite being disappointed, was actually flattered. "That's okay. I'm sure it happens all the time. Did you at least ... I mean, can I say I'm no longer a virgin?"

Now Roger's skin was *really* red. "Unfortunately no. I ... um ... 'finished' (he used air quotes when saying this) while I was putting on the condom." I suppose it would have been more accurate to have described this as Amy's almost-first time.

Just FYI, Roger left shortly after the incident, but not before explaining to Amy that although he was sure she had developed feelings for him, she should beware he was "not in the market for love." "Forget me as fast as you can," he told her. "You're gonna want to fall in love with me, but don't." Then, just as quickly as he came in, he stumbled out, never to be heard from again. The good news is Roger got his wish: Amy most certainly did not fall in love with him.

Can we get anything from Amy's tale? (Pun intended.) Actually, although her story could be construed as tragic, I think it was a blessing in disguise. One lesson here is that no matter how charming or sexy your local bartender/ waiter might be, it doesn't automatically mean they'll be great in bed. This story also proves premature ejaculation can sometimes be a good thing.

For the record, Amy didn't attempt any more one-night stands after her experience with Roger. Instead, she met a wonderfully nice man who was just fine with the notion of her falling in love with him. She did just that and they are now married with kids.

---

Neither John nor Amy were able to get too far in their quests. (Yeah, both crying and having sex with your condom are generally turn-offs.) But suppose they had completed their missions? As newbies to sex, would they have known what to do? I'm no Dr. Ruth and so I'll leave the more kinky conversation to her. But the *set-up* to a good sexual experience? *That* I know. Take a look:

## FIVE BASIC RULES FOR KISSING

I'm sure most of you scoff at the idea of needing kissing tips, but as someone who has kissed most of greater Los Angeles, I can assure you we all need some gentle reminders.

1. **Keep eye contact firm, but refrain from creepiness**: It's important to actually *look* at the person with whom you're going in for the kiss. (Don't just close your eyes and press your lips against theirs.) However, don't keep your eyes wide open like Malcolm McDowell in the *A Clockwork Orange* "conditioning" scene, because that might be a little scary. Feel free to engage in a little sweet and/or dirty talk, but be careful not to cross that cheesy line. Like please don't utter such things as: "Hey there, hot-stuff ..." at any time during the make-out process. It's disturbing and annoying and just plain wrong.

2. **Stay clean and minty!** Yeah, hey, it might be a good idea to pop in a breath mint every now and again. If nothing else, it will alleviate your concerns of having questionable breath, which leaves you freer to just be sexy. Tip: Listerine makes a great strip that simply melts on the tongue and is easy to carry around. There's no reason you shouldn't have this (or something comparable) with you at all times, except maybe when you're naked.

3. **Easy with that tongue.** It can be difficult to strike the perfect balance between too much tongue action and too little. Sometimes it's a matter of simply paying attention to your partner's kissing style and trying to adapt. (Like for example, make sure your tongue jewelry doesn't clash. If you have a fishhook in your tongue and she/he has a loop, who knows what could happen?) But let me just say this about the tongue: use it, but don't overdo it. I'm serious, people; there's no reason for you to shove your tongue down someone's throat, nor is it acceptable to flick it in and out of

a mouth as though you were a snake. In fact, if you're even thinking about what to do with your tongue, you're probably doing it wrong. It should naturally seek out your lover's mouth as you ease into the kiss.

**4** **Switch it up!** You know kissing isn't just about the tongue and it doesn't always have to be consistent. Keep things interesting with your partner by changing it up a bit. You could gently bite or suck on his lower lip or even give a subtle lick to the outside of his lips. Just so long as you don't simply mash your face up to your partner's, you're on the right track.

**5** **Your lover's mouth isn't your personal spit cup:** So one time I made out with this guy in the backseat of his Corvette. Not only was it the sloppiest kiss I'd ever received (and this includes kisses from basset hounds) but he never let me come up for air. Men do produce more saliva than women, but both genders have committed this wet-kiss crime. Be aware of how much you're salivating and try swallowing every now and then. Also, yes, it's pretty important to remember that no matter how kinky they are, everyone likes to breathe.

Even if you ignore all these tips, the only person who needs to love your kissing style is the person you're kissing. So while you might find these hints helpful, try not to over-think it. Just kiss.

When we were in high school (or for me, through my 20s) many of us referred to sexual activity as "the bases." It varied from town to town and clique to clique, but the way I learned it was: First base equaled kissing. Second base equaled feeling around *over* the clothes. Third base equaled feeling around *under* the clothes and, well, we all knew what a home run was.

I bring this up because those young folks who subscribed to the "bases" were actually onto something. Unless you're in a "wham, bam, thank you ma'am" scenario, it's important to remember that you can't just run straight for home plate.

## FIVES BASIC RULES FOR FOREPLAY

**1 Set the mood**: We don't want to go into cheese-mode. Like for example, please don't put leopard sheets on your round, rotating bed, and under no circumstances should you put on a Kenny G record. You're trying to *seduce* your partner, not shoot a porno in 1972. However, a little mellow music (think Radiohead or any emo Brit band, really) couldn't hurt. Also you don't have to run around the room lighting candles, as that can look a bit contrived, but do make sure your place is clean and inviting.

**2 Take it slow:** The main purpose of foreplay is to build sexual tension so that by the time you're ready for "real" sex, your bodies and minds are good and prepared. So, ya know, have your clothes on when you get started. If you're naked at the very beginning of the night, you won't have far to go (and plus most restaurants won't let you in without clothes). Don't rush into anything, and feel free to take your time with each step. Feel it out. If your partner seems resistant to move forward, never push it.

**3 No robots allowed:** While it's a good idea to take it slowly, try not to think of each "base" as a separate step. For example, you don't want a guy's inner monologue to be, "I'm kissing her, I'm kissing her, now I'm feeling her left boob, now it's time to go for the right one." You want everything to flow and not be over-analyzed (even though I clearly get that's what I'm doing in this chapter).

**4 Don't be too grabby:** Okay, first let me address the men here. When it comes time for a little breast feel, please don't grab it as though it were a rubber stress ball. I can't tell you how many times I've enjoyed a kiss when suddenly it felt like my boob was being crushed into a mammogram machine. Now, same goes for the ladies. I know you might be excited, but that's no reason to rush into the squeezing of the testes. Assuming you want your man to *remain* a man, you'll go easy. Of course, everyone will have different preferences, but I think it's safe to assume that no one wants a hospital visit right before sex.

**5 Keep talking!** I once made out with a guy who was turned on by discussing mundane moments of the day. Like, for example, he got totally hot when I described how I bleached the bathtub with Clorox or how I'd paid some bills online. That was kind of odd, I'll grant you, and when I say keep the line of communication open, I don't necessarily mean to that extent. But a little bit of dirty talk before and during sex never really hurt anyone.

**FAKING IT:** Ladies, you may choose to fake your enjoyment level sometimes, to put it delicately. And while I don't think you should make this a habit, as it doesn't really serve anyone in the end, if you feel on a particular occasion that you must fake it, for example, if you have an appointment to keep and your man's not gonna stop till he finishes the job and you know it ain't happening … please tone it down a notch. I have a neighbor who I'm sure is faking orgasms every night and it sounds like a Thai brothel in there. How do I know she's faking? The walls are so thin I could hear her on the phone (while her lover was, presumably, out of earshot) saying, "I just faked a good one." Yeah, well done, Meryl Streep. If only there was an Oscar for shortchanging yourself.

All right, so you're fumbling and stumbling around, trying to figure it all out as you go. Personally, nearly everything *I* ever learned on the subject of sex was from Judy Blume novels. In fact, here's a little side story: In fourth grade I smuggled Blume's book *Forever* onto a Girl Scout camping trip. Every night once our "leader" had gone to bed, I would gather the young girls around my Snoopy sleeping bag and read to them passages from the particularly dirty parts. We espe-

cially liked when the Michael character named his Johnson: "Ralph." Oh the hilarity! We laughed harder at this than when Tanya Reeder-man (not her real name) cried after seeing a picture of Cha-ka from *Land of the Lost*.

So night after night (after practic-ing the art of making

the perfect S'more) I regaled the young girls with chapters about people far beyond our years. I was their little sex-guru, which is painfully ironic seeing as how sex grossed me out until my 20s. But it all came to a screeching halt when our "leader" happened to wake up and catch me in the act. She said (and I remember this well) "I am appalled by your behavior, young lady." (I guess she too was grossed out by sex.) She confiscated the book and yelled, "That's warning #2, Ms. Knobler. One more and you're going home." (Warning #1 came after I insisted to her that I didn't speak or understand English and instead could only communicate using "Jive-speak.")

Since that week I have never been camping again, but I do always chuckle when hearing the name "Ralph," which only reinforces the conclusion that we are extremely impressionable as nine-year-olds.

This leads me to a whole other memory, which I will now share. A little before the Girl Scout/Judy Blume incident, my mother began teaching disco dancing in our converted garage. Now, here are three facts you should know: 1) It was the late 1970s 2) This converted garage was also our playroom, so in order for these lessons to take place, all of my Barbies had to be pushed off to the side 3) We lived in Waco, Texas. That's right: Waco, Barbies, disco and my mother; all things you probably wouldn't naturally put in the same sentence. But this *was* the 1970s, so bear with me.

I recall entering this playroom/garage on one particularly humid day, in search of my Donny Osmond doll. (It had purple socks!) I didn't know my mother's students had already arrived and when I opened the door, I was shocked to see there were two men doing the tango. One of them (we'll call him Jacques) even had a rose in his mouth, which was especially odd seeing as how we didn't have rose bushes. (It was also odd that during disco lessons they were doing the tango, but technically class hadn't officially begun.)

What does this have to do with sex, you might be asking? Well, I'll tell you it has *everything* to with sex. Because for the first time, I saw with my own eyes two people actually *flirting* with one another in a way that I knew was different from Donny and Marie. (For some reason, I thought Donny and Marie were husband and wife until about 1992.) Yes of course my own parents had sat closely on the living-room couch, but they were far past the courting stage once I'd come along.

No, here were two people, Jacques and Wilhelm (again, not his real name) who either had a history together or wanted to *make* history together. And while I didn't see this as being anything risqué, it was here I learned that sex, if you're lucky, is born out of chemistry between any combination of genders. "It's not just for Donny and Marie," I exclaimed loudly. The group of dancers laughed and asked if I'd like to learn the YMCA dance, but my mother soon arrived to scoot me out of the room.

In case anyone is wondering, shortly after that day, nearly everyone in that disco class got cast in a Waco Civic Theater production of *Oklahoma*. Wilhelm looked especially handsome in his cowboy hat. It was another five years before I learned that even if I *were* an adult, he'd probably not want to marry me.

## I MEANT IT AT THE TIME

Sex and sexual attraction is a funny thing. Whatever level of importance we place on it varies so greatly from person to person and from situation to situation that it's difficult to determine the "norm." I can only *really* understand it through my own eyes and this much I know: the importance I place on sex hasn't always gelled with my now-ex-lovers.

As you might imagine, Slug wasn't the only man I've slept with for whom it meant a tad more to me than to him. This isn't to say I've never had boyfriends who loved me or valued our intimacy. Let's just say it hasn't *always* been the case. But I'll give Slug this much: at least he didn't operate from a false pretense. He got in and out without writing me vacuous sonnets full of empty promises. In fact, come to think of it, the only thing Slug ever promised was to not sleep with any of my sorority sisters if we ever broke up. (I'm not sure he actually kept that promise, but that's something to ponder another day.)

This was in sharp contrast with a guy we'll call Dillon, a man I met shortly after Slug and I split. *Dillon's* the one who pulled out all the stops. We'd worked together on our college campus, living in close quarters. He'd often leave plush stuffed animals and tulips outside of my dorm room. One day, he knocked on the door and when I opened it, he'd left a basket of cornbread and some Dallas Cowboys bumper stickers. Seeing as how I was a Texan living in D.C., he figured (correctly) that this was truly the way to my heart.

I took one look at that blue and white football helmet pained on the sticker and knew that Dillon and I would make out in the near future. It only took a few hours. That same night, he just happened to show up at the nearby dance club I frequented and at some point during "Baby Got Back," he kissed me and we fell in love. (I guess there really *is* something magical about Sir Mix-A-Lot.)

He continued to court me for the next month, and even though sex was new to me I didn't need much more from him to know that I wanted us to sleep together. One frosty Washington night, we did just that and everything changed. At last, I was sleeping with someone with whom I was madly in love and I could *finally* see what all the fuss was about! Everything was different because sex had become so much more than just a story to share with my friends. It was now the physical expression of pure love … or at least that's what I thought.

For Dillon it wasn't quite the same. Now to be fair to myself, he *did* look me straight in the eye and tell me he loved me. I mean sure, I'd said it first and it took him a good 24 hours to return the sentiment. In fact, it had been so long between my first admission of love and his that when he finally said, "I love you too," I thought he was talking about the band U2. I think I then said something like, "Yes, Bono is wonderful," which is an odd thing to say during sex, unless of course you're Bono.

The point is at that time, for me, sex meant everything. For him, it was fun. See the difference? I learned of this discrepancy when he broke up with me two-and-a-half months later to date a very large redhead whom you may remember from a previous chapter as the "girl who wore Jellies."

When I kicked and screamed, "But you *said*! You said you *loved* me!" He replied with those six little words that sting like Botox injections: "I meant it at the time." And there it is. Because he did probably mean it at the time, as sex makes us feel or at least think we feel everything at a highly intense level. Once the glow of it all has lifted, those "intense feelings" start to fade like old photos and we're left with a mixed-up mess of therapy invoices.

Of course, I realize that not all sex is a product of being in a relationship, and there might be wild nights when neither gender overanalyzes. And sure, anyone might exaggerate his or her emotions in the heat of passion. There's the "you're the best I've ever had" exclamation. I mean, can we really *scientifically* examine that? How can that be proven? I once had a guy scream, "Let's get married!" during sex. Yeah, *there's* an awkward follow-up. And of course, don't forget the "I love you's" that perhaps only one of you (or none or both) really meant at the time.

I can't speak for men and can only report on what I've seen, but along with the man's strong post-coital feeling of wanting to sleep, his strong feelings during the climax seem to want to slumber too. We women, on the other hand, can get so jazzed up by this intimacy we want to snuggle and chat and get *closer*. We assign meaning to something that might have been there for 30 minutes, but isn't there now.

But all is not lost here, as long as women understand that sex isn't *every-thing* and men understand that sex isn't *nothing*. But keep in mind that along with the morning sun, our issues come flooding back. So now let's get back to the relationship stuff, blemishes and all.

"Love isn't love until it's past."

– Prince

For me, college was a place for first-times. It was the first time I had sex, the first time I ever really grasped my social security number, the first time I did beer bongs, the first time I had a real boyfriend who wasn't fabricated in my head and, subsequently, the first time I ever lost said boyfriend. (And no, it wasn't Slug.) I was wrecked, and because I'd never experienced real heartbreak before, I felt like I'd reached a level of despair never experienced by a fellow human being.

Of course that was a ridiculous notion, but when we're experiencing first times, we assume our emotions are the first to reach such intensity. I recall calling my mom from my dorm room, sobbing as though I'd just found my husband of 30 years in bed with another woman. The truth was, I'd just been dumped by a dorky frat-boy after we'd dated for a mere two months. "I … (sob) … he … (sob) … why?"

My mother, after quoting her usual lyrics from Neil Diamond's "Love on the Rocks," said the following: "You throw your love around like you hate it. You need to chill out and relax. Have a cocktail."

That struck me. Not the part about needing a cocktail, because that's always been fairly obvious. No, the "I throw my love around like I hate it" line. It was true. For something so precious as love, I was awfully careless with it, as though it were just a pen I stole from the bank. "No, you just keep it. I'll get another one." And not only have *I* had to suffer because of this, so have my poor, dear friends.

Case in point: this first college breakup. After two frenetic months together, he decided to move on and out came my Barbra Streisand CDs. I mean, *really* ... what college student in the 1990s even *had* Barbra Streisand CDs? I did, and I played them nonstop. "When I wake up each morning trying to find myself," Babs droned through my roommate's cheap, tiny speakers. Why did I relate to *that*? I woke up each morning trying not to vomit from the Jello shots I'd done the night before; I hardly had time to "find myself."

She went on, "I did my best to keep you satisfied." Did I *really* do my best to keep him "satisfied," or did I merely invite him to a few Alpha Epsilon Phi semi-formals? Could *this* have been what Barbra was singing about?

But the worst of it was that my lovely friends had to hear about it incessantly. After the third month of my being unable to function as a human being, they were at a loss. One of them even bought me a huge bouquet of yellow happy-face balloons, which temporarily cheered me up until I realized one of the balloons bore a slight resemblance to the guy who'd broken up with me. My friend responded, "I don't really see how they look alike," and I'd snapped back, "It's the *eyes*. You don't *see* that?"

I'd really like to say I finally got over this guy who looked like a happy-face balloon, but I'm not sure I ever did. However, I did live to tell about it and have still more stories to share. So here we go ...

# CHAPTER 8

# The Split

Let me begin by sharing a few of my pals' inspirational and "favorite" break-up tales. What better to start with than another story of my very own?

## ALAN AND HIS ALASKAN ADVENTURE

I'd met Alan in my early 20s at some rundown bar in West Hollywood. He was a tad older, a musician (of course) and had beautiful green eyes (oddly the exact color of my yoga mat). We hit it off immediately and started officially dating the following week.

After about seven months of blissful courtship, Alan got a job as the resident Spanish guitar player on a cruise ship. Destination: Alaska! The gig called for him to pack his bags (and guitar, of course) for a three-month, nonstop stint. I was devastated, but Alan assured me that we would remain together and that the distance and short time apart would help our "love" to grow. We'd write, we'd call, we'd miss each other so dearly that nothing, not even Princess Cruises, could come between us. Well.

Since Al wouldn't have his official mailing address until he arrived on the boat, the plan was that he'd call or write when he got there with the information. (This was pre-Internet.) One week went by, then two, then three. I'd taken up the habit of literally pacing around my dingy apartment, attempting to *will* the phone to ring with my desperation. It didn't.

After four weeks, I got a postcard that said on its cover, "Greetings from Juno." It had a little picture of a white polar bear sliding around on some ice. I turned it over and guess what Al had written as the first line. "Greetings from Juno!" Um, hadn't we already covered that in the postcard photo? Did he really need to waste a whole line of this very tiny letter reiterating that he was in Alaska and that he wanted to "*greet*" me?

It got worse. After that, he went on and on about how gorgeous Alaska was, and how he never, ever wanted to come home. *Wha?* There was no mention of "missing me" or "wanting me to visit" or even "wanting me" at all. I was crushed.

'Fine,' I thought. 'He's just really busy and wants to live in "the now." It will all be right as rain just as soon as he gets back.' I did what any 22-year-old smitten young woman would do. I wrote him a poem. I luckily don't still have a copy of it, but I'm pretty sure it involved comparing his eyes to the green hills of Malibu (which, if I stop to think about it, totally doesn't make sense).

I mailed him the poem and waited anxiously for a few more weeks, when at last came another postcard. This time it had a picture of a moose sniffing some grass near an apple tree (I assume just waiting to be popped off by Sarah Palin). Al wrote, "Hope this letter finds you well. All is wonderful on this boat and Charlotte and I find ourselves wandering the lovely wilderness on the rare occasion we get time off." CHARLOTTE? HUH?!?! "She's loads of fun. Anyway, hope L.A. is treating you well."

WHO THE F$%K WAS CHARLOTTE? And why was he just casually plopping her name into the postcard? Now I was floored. I wrote back another poem, something about his long guitar-playing fingers, and then P.S.'d it, "Hey, who's Charlotte?"

It took him only a week and half to reply, this time with a real letter instead of just a card. My heart raced as I tore it open with the anticipation of an answer I did not want. But no answer came. Instead, Al just used a longer forum to once again describe the beauty of Alaska and discuss the wonderful adventures with "Charlotte."

After this, a series of postcards came about every five days, simply detailing the love that was blooming between him and Charlotte. He made no mention of my poem or the fact that we had ever even dated. Just letter after letter, talking about how he might just stay up north, as he's sick of the L.A. music scene.

Eventually the letters stopped, and after a few months I never heard from Al again. Even though technically I wasn't "broken up" with, I felt the break and I was mortified. There was no closure, no acknowledgment, no nothing. So either Al actually *forgot* I'd been his girlfriend or he just couldn't deal. I'd bet the boat it was the latter.

## DANNY'S BIG YANKEE IDEA

So this next breakup story *almost* happened, but luckily it was thwarted in the nick of time. My buddy Danny had been dating a woman we'll call Sue for about three years. Like most, the relationship had its ups and downs, but the final eight months had been almost all downs. A mutual friend had relayed to Dan that Sue was cheating on him with a co-worker and Dan wanted out. But as someone who wasn't great with confrontation, he just didn't know how to end it. He admitted he tried to do that thing guys do wherein they act like complete a-holes in order to get the woman to break up with *them*. (Later on we'll discuss that further.)

Sue didn't get it. She wanted to work through their issues, not realizing that Dan already had one foot out. And so he decided he would give her the news in a *big* way. His brother had proposed to his current wife using the JumboTron at a college football game. (Hook 'em horns!) Even though it was a bit of a cliché to use this method, it hadn't failed to impress Dan's brother's wife and seemed to be a big hit with the crowd. Dan thought, "Well, if people can use the JumboTron for proposals of marriage, why can't they use it for proposals of breaking up?" (Awful, I know.)

He and Sue had tickets for a Yankees game and he knew a guy who knew a guy who could make it happen. Dan wrote the whole breakup speech out and was just about to submit it for the big screen when he received information from his "source" that Sue was *not* having an affair. (The source had gotten her confused with another woman in the office by the same name.)

So here's what happened. Dan, after hearing the news, began to think that perhaps there *was* still something there between him and Sue. He sold the Yankees tickets and instead took her out for an expensive, romantic dinner. They were about halfway through the second course and Sue had been yammering on an on about how she was "sick of Rebecca from accounting." It was at this point Dan realized he didn't care if she was having an affair. He still wanted to dump her.

He *did* at least wait until they'd gotten home to break up with Sue the normal way and, although she was very hurt, at least he didn't opt to do it through a fortune cookie.

## THE CASE OF THE FROSTY WINDOW

Here's one of my favorites. A guy, let's say Marcus, went over to his girlfriend's (whom we'll call Jenny) New York apartment late one Tuesday night. They'd been dating for 10 months and as far as Jenny knew, things seemed to be going well. So you'll understand her surprise when she learned Marcus was breaking up with her.

He gave her a relatively well-prepared speech and she cried, and he cried, and they cried together for at least an hour. Finally it was time for Marcus to make his final departure. He (still crying) kissed her on the forehead and said something ridiculous like "I wish you joy." He left and Jenny immediately put on a sad Fiona Apple record and decided to stare out the window in order to (melodramatically) watch Marcus leave, one last time.

Through her own tears and the heart-crushing sound of Fiona's piano, Jenny wiped away some frost on the window and leaned her head forward to watch her beloved. And lo and behold, what did she see? Marcus was skipping down the sidewalk. Literally skipping. Guess he wasn't all that torn up about it.

Oddly, this helped Jenny get over Marcus in about half the time it would otherwise have taken her. How he faked his tears, she'll never know.

## HOW WE HANDLE BREAKUPS

If you're with me on our original premise that women *can* (not always) lean a little nutty and men have been known to (not always) get tangled up in lies, nothing exemplifies those attributes more than a breakup. I speculate that women perhaps have a tendency to go a little nutty *because* men lie, and men lie because women have that tendency. And alas, the cycle continues.

## THE OL' MAKE 'EM HATE YOU ROUTINE

This tactic was used by about half of the guys who have ever dumped me, and it really seems to be a guy thing. It goes like this: One party in the relationship (for the sake of this vignette we'll call him Jack) wants to break up with his girlfriend. (Let's just use the name Cecilia.) But Jack doesn't want to be the "bad guy." (Or more likely, he's just too chicken to deal with it.)

So what does Jack do? Jack acts like a douche bag. If all goes according to Jack's plan, Cecilia becomes so angry and disillusioned with him, she wants out too, and dumps him. Then Jack gets what he wants (out of the relationship) while also enjoying his status as a victim. Meanwhile, he never had to make the big dreaded speech.

Here's how I have dealt with *my* Jacks. I simply don't break up with them. Sure, it's an immature move and it causes just as much suffering for me as it does for him. But because I *know* what he's up to, I kind of find it enjoyable to watch him squirm. As I type this, I realize it sounds crazy, but hey, no apologies. Besides, read the title of this book.

This game can be loads of fun. I dated one guy for a while, and near the end he was trying everything he could to get me to break up with him. He literally said to me one Sunday morning, "Hey, Cec, looks like you put on some weight." I was fuming but instead of giving in to his passive-aggressive bullshit, I said: "Aw, Petey. You're in a grouchy mood cuz you haven't had enough *sun* today. Aw, Grouchy Petey-Pete."

Same thing happened with an ex I'll call Ben. I knew he'd been trying to dump me for months but for some reason, crazy me, I pretended not to notice. One night while he was in the shower, he left his computer on and opened to a word document. In a large, bolded font, he'd written, "FOR NICKI'S EYES ONLY." Of course I had to read further and discovered the following note. "Hi Nicki … lied to Cecily again today. She thinks I was on the phone all night with Jason. See ya soon, Love Ben."

Instead of confronting him, I said, "Hey Ben, you accidentally left your word document up. Don't worry, I didn't read it." This infuriated him. His plan wasn't working and he soon realized he was gonna have to man-up and do the breaking-up. If I was going to be the dumpee, I at least wanted to be in a position to pity myself. It was only fair.

The glaring problem with the "make them break up with you" scheme is this: not only is it passive aggressive, it's also cruel. The breakup will occur sooner or later, which will be painful in itself. But this way of doing it might also emotionally scar the person you're dumping. There's no need to drag anyone's heart through the mud.

Sure sometimes people who want out of a relationship get testy and their frustration is played out on their partner. But if you care enough about a person to have formed a relationship that must be broken up from, you should respect that person sufficiently to be honest and up front.

(Side note: Ben and Nicki did end up dating, but they broke up when Nicki allegedly realized she was a lesbian. Oh sweet universe.)

## IT'S NOT YOU, IT'S ME ...
## SERIOUSLY, IT'S ME – I LOATHE YOU

Surely you've heard the "it's not you, it's me" speech. (I know I've heard it dozens of times.) Both men and women use it, but as a tactic, it's representative of the female brain.

As instinctual nurturers, women lean toward protecting emotions. Because we don't want loved ones to hurt, we insist we're ending a relationship because of our *own* deficiencies, as opposed to *their* flaws. "It's not you, it's me! I'm all f#$ked up. I just need to figure *my* stuff out before I can be good for anyone."

As I mentioned, men use this speech a lot too and, in fact, I called a guy out on it once. He had said something like, "Really, it's me. Not you. You're amazing. You're wonderful and beautiful and it's totally not you." With a genuinely confused face, I replied, "Wait, so it's *you*? You *hate* amazing and wonderful and beautiful people? Aw, well *that* makes sense!" One time I desperately wanted to say to a guy, "It's not you, it's me. It's totally me. I'm just weird because I don't like guys who live in their parent's basement. *You're* great. *I'm* really screwed up because I guess I just don't like basements. Or your parents. I'm gonna work on that!"

Women, when giving this break-up speech, often add the dreaded phrase, "You're a really nice guy." They'll say something along the lines of: "It's not you, it's me. You're such a nice guy and I must be a moron." Men might read this as "So chicks don't like nice guys?" which is unfortunate because that's certainly not a lesson we'd like to teach.

The truth is, while it may sound cliché, "It's not you, it's me" can indeed soften the blow a little. We might feel less down on ourselves if given the chance to think: "Well maybe it's *not* me. Maybe it's this guy/girl who's all screwed up," even if we've said this before to past lovers and it doesn't totally ring true. While the statement may be utter baloney, it gives us a chance to save face. Besides, matters of the heart rarely follow protocol, and perhaps sometimes we recognize that we really are doing something stupid when breaking up with someone. In other words, we honestly believe the person we're breaking up with is a great catch, albeit for someone else, and that the problem indeed lies with us and not them.

One problem with this tactic is it can give false hope. The person being dumped thinks the dumper really cares and that there might be a chance down the line once his/her baggage is dealt with. While this is always *possible*, it's highly unlikely. Maybe it would be okay to simply say, "I have had a good time with you and you're a wonderful person, but I'm just not feeling this as a long-term possibility." Or even something along the lines of, "You know what? It's not you and it's not me. We're both great. It's just not right."

There's very little anyone can say to make the pain of breaking up less deep. But being genuine and respectful can ultimately help you both heal faster because you can hopefully skip the whole phase of hating one another. Isn't that a nice concept?

### THE "OH, ARE WE STILL DATING?" EXIT STRATEGY

This tactic is similar to the "make 'em hate you" method and actually often accompanies it. I don't know whether this approach comes more often from men or women, but based on the folks in *my* circle of acquaintances, it seems to be a guy thing.

So let's say you want out, but you just can't bring yourself to give the speech. What do you do? You move on with your life without telling the person you're seeing. Oops! Remember my story about Alan the musician in Alaska? The one who simply "forgot to break up with me" before moving on to another woman? This was clearly his tactic of choice.

Now, this can go down one of two ways. Either the dumper begins an affair with another person (also known as cheating) until as time passes he (we'll just say he) spends more and more time with the other woman and less and less time with you, until at some point the cheating relationship becomes the real one. This would be pretty much what happened with Alan. The other

way is that he simply stops calling and pretends he never knew you. I knew a woman in Texas who was *married* for 11 years and one day her husband (hell of a guy) moved all his stuff out and disappeared. She had thought they were perfectly happy and then boom ... she never heard from him again.

This method is unusually cruel, selfish and immature. Not only does it take away the right of the woman being dumped to respond in any way to this person she's shared part of her life with, it almost negates the whole relationship. And if cheating *is* involved, it's a betrayal unlike no other. This is the most unacceptable way to end a relationship, no matter how volatile you may have deemed it. Hear that, "Alan?"

## THE "I CAN'T HEAR YOU, I'M GOING THROUGH A CANYON" RUSE

Here's one I'm not especially proud of, but I *have* once or twice made it difficult for a guy to break up with me by pretending my phone was cutting out during his big speech. One guy called me at home on my landline. When he began his descent into breakup territory, I said something like, "Oops, I'm going through the canyon and you're cutting out." Even though he'd called me at home, he somehow believed me and kept repeating himself as though I couldn't hear him. Eventually, he drove over to my place to deliver the speech in person and, I suppose, to find out exactly what kind of canyon runs through my kitchen.

## THE CO-DEPENDENT BREAKUP STANDOFF

Here's an oldie but goodie: the couple who simply can't call it off. By definition this can't be more common in one gender or another. In this scenario both people in the relationship are way over it and yet have gotten so comfortable, either in their boredom or their routine, they just can't leave it behind.

If you recognize yourself in this category, please don't feel ashamed. It's completely normal. We've all done this at one time or another. In a way, the fact that you stay in a relationship after it's no longer really working is a positive testament to your character – it means you feel a strong loyalty to your partner.

Or maybe it's just that you can't fathom the idea of being alone on a Saturday night. Whatever the reason, neither you *nor* your partner can call it quits.

Here's an example. (Wow, the amount of guys I've dated and been dumped by is somewhat unsettling, isn't it?) In my early 20s I realized about a week into a relationship with a particular guy that it was all wrong. He was adorably cute, very sweet and truly earnest. But he just didn't get me and I didn't get him. (Also he wore leather vests with no shirt underneath, but that's not the point.) He literally said to me once, "You have such a weird sense of humor. You say things that are absurd and aren't true with this weird *tone*. I don't get it." I asked myself, "How do you explain the concept of *sarcasm* to someone?" and could never find that answer.

But I felt like I was at fault. I thought, "Here is this cute, sweet guy who *wants* to be with me and *likes* dating me. And yet for some reason I don't feel the love I want to feel." And then of course I came to the ridiculous conclusion, "I just must not be able to feel love." So I stayed, and stayed, and tried, and tried until I looked up and it had been two years. When checking in with my feelings, again I thought, "This is *my* fault and I'm gonna stick it out."

And then something extraordinary happened. I fell in absolute, head-over-heels love with someone else. Now mind you, I'm not a believer in cheating,

and nothing happened until I broke up with Mr. Leather-Vest-Guy. But once I understood what real, thick, unrelenting love felt like, I knew that what I had been experiencing with my boyfriend was definitely not it.

Funnily enough, years later I found out Mr. Leather-Vest (whom I still maintain is a catch for one of you ladies out there) felt the same way. He *liked* me, he *respected* me, but the love simply wasn't there. After we broke up we remained friends, and he went on to meet a wonderful woman who a) wasn't annoyingly sarcastic and b) wasn't an a-hole snob (like me) when it came to wearing vests.

As for me, after the breakup I gave it a month of respectful mourning and then pursued my *real* love. You might remember him from a few chapters ago as the "left a letter to another girl onscreen for me to see" guy, so obviously things didn't work out. But I did love him and I am grateful he came along to show me what love was *supposed* to feel like.

Basically, when it doesn't feel right, it isn't. While no one likes to go through painful detachments, it's important that we never settle. Settling now will likely cause a much more painful breakup down the road. It's also a good idea to be truthful (that is, saying "I'm not totally feeling this"). In that case the other person might make the decision for both of you. Of course all relationships will have times when you feel uncertain or unsettled, and this doesn't always mean you should break up. What it *does* mean is that you should start to pay attention to what you really feel and to any problems that might be brewing. And, after giving it a good amount of thought and talking with your partner, you should act honestly on those feelings.

## DEALING WITH IT

We've discussed firsthand accounts of breakups and ways in which people end things. But what do we do once it's all over? How ever do we cope? Once again, men and women often differ when it comes to dealing with their hearts being ripped in half. Let's discuss a few potential reactions…

"I MEAN, I'M NOT GONNA BE *IGNORED*, DAN"
– Glenn Close as Alex Forrest in *Fatal Attraction*

The film *Fatal Attraction* put a bright red spotlight on the woman often referred to as the "psycho-chick." And in what event does the "psycho-chick" usually shine? That's right, The Break Up. Now I don't want anyone (women especially) to get upset with this term. And while *obviously* all women do not go on to be psycho-chicks while breaking up or otherwise, many of us can … maybe, on occasion … plead just a tad guilty to personifying this description.

In fact, indulge me in a liberating exercise. Admitting to having ever been the psycho-ex (woman *or* man) can free your soul. I'll start and I'll scream it from the proverbial rooftop. "I, Cecily Knobler, do declare that I have at one time (or two or three or four) been a psycho-chick." There, I feel better. Now *you* try. And if you truly can't remember a time when you were guilty of this, you're either amazingly balanced, lucky, or lying to yourself.

For me, the psycho qualities really come out only during the breakup. It hasn't seemed to matter if I dated the guy one month or three years; if I'm the one being dumped, I always lose it a little. Okay, a lot. (For the record, if I'm doing the breaking up, I'm surprisingly graceful.) I haven't spiraled *every* time, but let's just say there are few men out there who won't be adding me as a friend on Facebook.

Once I'm done making my breaker-upper wish he'd never been born, by for example, forcing him to have a 12-hour deconstruction of *why* we're breaking up, I usually feel a little better. (I think I once asked a guy whom I had dated for six weeks to take a polygraph test to prove he hadn't cheated. He respectfully declined.) I never do the drive-bys anymore and I try to avoid drunk dialing (although I have been known to send an Ambien-fueled text or two).

Try to pinpoint where your crazy tendencies come out (and again, if they don't, good for you). Is it during the relationship itself, during the breakup like me or in the months (years) after? Now just because I'm encouraging you to get in touch with your inner crazy doesn't mean you shouldn't strive to be better. The calmer and more respectfully you can conduct yourself, the better. But breakups are usually messy and ugly and the first thing to go (besides their number from your cell phone) is your dignity.

And I want to point out for a moment that it is never, *ever* okay to get physically or verbally abusive. The worst thing anyone can do during a fight or breakup, besides inflicting physical harm, is to lash out and say things that can't be retracted. If you are wise enough to refrain from doing this, you've probably encountered it and it's never pretty. Hurting someone because you're hurting absolutely never helps. (Nor does blocking the door, which I've learned the hard way.) The worst thing I ever said to someone during a breakup was "Your screenplays will never sell." I regretted it immediately and realized that, as sad and angry as I was, I still loved him and wanted him to be happy. (In case anyone cares, his scripts have not sold to date.)

## DENYING YOUR ANGER ONLY LEADS TO MORE ANGER

As someone who tends to let every emotion seep out of them for all to see, one breakup phenomenon has always intrigued me. It's the "everything's fine, nothing to see here" tactic, wherein the person being dumped (or at times the dumper) acts as though they have no resentment or lingering feelings toward their ex-partner.

This is not to say there aren't times in which people feel resolute in their decision to break up. In fact, often – especially for the dumper but even some-times the dumpee – there is a feeling of bittersweet (and sometimes *just* sweet) relief as they let go of something they feel wasn't working. But to act as though they have no doubts or feelings of sadness is usually a sign of denial, espe-cially if they invested a lot of time in the relationship.

In my experience this way of dealing is more common among men. If they're the ones ending it, they might immerse themselves in work or hard partying with their friends. They'll act as though there is absolutely nothing missing from their lives and may even take it to the extreme and act as if their ex never existed. I've seen guys (and yes, also some women) do this when they've been broken up with, as well. "Everything's fine; all is great … no one can hurt me" seems to be their motto.

The problems arise when the confusing feelings of resentment, guilt and just plain sadness from the detachment get stuffed into the far corners of the psyche. What happens when deep, dark emotions get repressed? They come

out in other ways. The individual is likely to overcompensate by developing self-destructive behavior (for example, having sex with everything that moves).

What I've seen time and again is that when this anger and sadness is not dealt with, it carries over to the next relationship. Many refer to this as "baggage." I call it the "Russian-doll complex." The term baggage implies that we carry our bullshit from our past in a suitcase for all to see. But with a Russian doll, everything stays hidden, sometimes deep within other layers, until someone persistent comes along and brings it all out of hiding ... or until the doll explodes and the madness all comes out at once.

It's nearly impossible not to carry *some* stuff from one relationship to the next, but hopefully the lessons are mainly constructive and will help the new relationship rather than hurt it. So next time you're on either end of a breakup, make sure you sufficiently explore your feelings. Even though it might hurt at the time, it should pay off in the long run.

## PLAYING DUMB

Here's one of my favorite things to do ever (and you can all try this at home sometime when you're bored). This little gem takes years to perfect, but this is what I do: I call guys who broke up with me, say six to eight years ago, and say the following: "Hey, it's me!" Pause while they try to figure out who I am. "Cecily! Anyway, so ... are we *good*? I mean, are we moving forward with this? Because you said you needed some space and I feel I *gave* that to you, but I can't wait forever."

Yeah, guys (and I'm sure women) absolutely love this. I did this recently with Ben, knowing full well he's now married. Just called him up and pretended I thought we had been on "a break" these past seven years. I acted as though the last time we'd talked (which we hadn't since the breakup) he'd said he needed time to think and figure out what he wanted and that I'd been waiting this whole time for him to "get back to me." He laughed nervously and finally told me it was officially over.

This one is especially fun because you get to do something crazy without really *appearing* crazy. Who cares what your ex thinks? Invite a few buddies over, make a martini and go for it. But be warned: you must be fully over your ex for this to be humorous, as otherwise it might be a bit sad. And don't be mean to your ex. The goal of this isn't to mock him (or get a restraining order for yourself). The point is to prove to yourself you can finally make light of something that was once so dark.

## MAGICAL REVENGE

Just when you think there couldn't possibly be a man left in this world I hadn't dated, here's another. I, for a good amount of time, dated the host of a popular reality show. I won't say which one, but I will admit it's a program that has a high preference on my TiVo settings. I will also tell you it was *American Idol*. Oops.

He got cast just a few months after we'd broken up for, oh let's say the third time. (By the way, he left the show after the first season because of what he called "creative differences," so he's not the host you're thinking of.) Now I'm not here to slam him and so I won't. I will admit, however, that I not-so-secretly wished I could have used my touchtone telephone to have him voted off my television.

Now, having to see your recent ex's face on billboards does not make it easier to heal. I'll admit I was more at a loss than usual. And so I did what any young 20-something woman might do. I went to the nearest new-age bookstore to purchase a book on hexing.

At first it was a joke. I'd gone in and asked the lovely hippie where I might find a book or pamphlet on "spells." She asked, the violet crystals on her necklace sparkling ever so brightly in the sun, "Oh, do you mean spells for bringing love into your life? Or perhaps you'd like a success spell. They're very popular right now. You can find them right over …"

I cut her off. "No, I'm actually looking to f#$% somebody's life up pretty good. Do you have anything for that?"

She appeared disappointed in me, which frankly I'd expected. "Well, if that's *really* what you're looking for, we have a 'Black Magic' section over there. Although to be honest, I don't condone it."

"Thanks," I said, and the unwilling friend I'd brought with me and I both laughed and headed toward the section. After flipping through at least five books, I returned to the front counter to make my purchase and continue my conversation with the hippie. "This one seems perfect. Oh hey, also, do you

know where I might be able to get the tail of a rhesus monkey and … a lock of Alan Thicke's hair? This here spell says I might need those…"

Not making eye contact, she replied, "I'm sorry. I can't and won't help you."

I never did use that spell book (and for the record, don't even believe in such things). I eventually got over my anger and ultimately wished this guy well so I'm glad I never attempted to put a curse on him. Plus, the idea of having to cut a piece of Alan Thicke's hair seemed quite daunting.

## THE GRAY ZONE

Last, but certainly not least common, is the tendency for couples who break up to enter into a different kind of relationship with far less defined boundaries. Some call it "exes with benefits" (a variation on the popular "friends with benefits," which we'll talk about in the next chapter) and some just use that all-inclusive term "f$%k-buddies." Whatever term you choose to use, I can unequivocally report that *it doesn't work*!

Some people feel that continuing to sleep with their jilted ex will help them to make an easier transition from "together" to "apart." In reality, it only confuses intimate feelings and worse, it can confuse expectations, especially for the person on the receiving end of the breakup.

I know I've been guilty of believing I could turn my ex around by having sex with him one more time. Like many, I confused sex with love and believed I could somehow remind my ex how wonderful it had all been. What I failed to consider was that they broke it off *for a reason*. And once the morning hits, in my experience, the sex has been forgotten like a trip to McDonald's. Sadly one person (in this case, me) is left wondering what it all means. "Are we back together? Does he still love me? Would he sleep here if he didn't?" And the other (in this example, him) is left thinking: "Bonus lay. Cool. Hmm, what's for breakfast?"

It's nearly impossible for men and women to be on the same page at all times. But it's almost guaranteed that their perspectives will be far apart if they attempt to go from a romantic sexual relationship to a "just friendly" sexual relationship. One person is bound to expect more than the other, whether it's an intimacy issue, commitment confusion or both. And you can count on the fact that at least one person will be hurt all over again.

This absolutely doesn't mean you can't stay friends with your exes (in fact, I'm not sure I'd have many friends if I didn't). However, you'll normally need some time and distance to make that transition. Not showing up at their apartment at 3:00 am also helps.

## BUT NOW I SEE

If you haven't yet had the misfortune of being dumped (and most of us have) I can only describe it as a mesh of mental and physical uneasiness. Every organ, every muscle, every *everything* just feels off, as if it's been tweaked slightly to the left and needs adjusting. For me, my lungs can't quite seem to catch up with the speed at which I'm breathing. My heart feels like it can't properly transfer blood or oxygen from one chamber to the other. There's a little spot just below the breastbone but above the stomach, and with especially bad breakups, that spot feels hollow like no amount of food or sleep or compassion or even yellow happy-face balloons can fill it.

In other words, it sucks. Whether you're coming out of an intense two-month romance with the dorkiest classmate or a four-year relationship that has been slowly dying, it's never easy to have someone *in* your life and then just *out*. And that, my dears, is why there have been countless songs, poems and even movies completely devoted to the breakup. Let me reiterate, I've been there so many times it has become *almost* comical. I've been dumped on vacation, via text messaging and on cell-phone voicemails. I even once got broken up with through an instant message on my laptop. But the thing is, breakups have this beautiful way of freeing us from someone who clearly wasn't giving us his all.

We can all strive to handle things better, but when push comes to shove, it's easier said than done. Here I am writing about it and yet I can't seem to stop blocking doors or sleeping with the ex. What I *can* tell you is that with each experience, I learn to handle things just a little bit better. (I'm sure there are lots of boys from my early dating days who would rather have met me later in life.) If you pay attention to your pattern of reaction, you too can get healthier with each go-around.

So let's end this breakup chapter with some hopefully positive words: nothing brings your appreciation of friends out more than the ending of a relationship. Make sure you reach out to those friends when you're hurting and keep yourself busy. (For example, watching 15 episodes of *The Real World/Road Rules Challenge* in a row, which is the type of thing I would do, might Zen out the brain, but it could also instill a deeper loneliness.) As much as you might want to shut down and shut in, force yourself to have a plan with a buddy at

least once a week. From there, it can grow to a few times a week and pretty soon, you'll find yourself back in a healthy routine. You will get over your breakups. Or your TiVo will shut down and force you to leave the house. Either way, you will survive.

"… and it's all too much hindsight"

– Death Cab for Cutie

If I could go back to age 15 and hand myself a note moments before I laid my eyes on Patrick, I would. (Remember Patrick from the first chapter?) And in that note, I would write the following message: "This won't matter." Of course it's difficult to explain to a freshman in high school that young infatuations are merely blips on their screen of life. But I wish somehow I could have convinced *me* not to waste too much time pining after a senior with a big ego and little love to requite. I'd also tell high-school me not to wear parachute pants and spiked belts.

I suppose we do have to experience these lessons for ourselves in order to truly appreciate and learn from them. But what if we could get just a little head start? What advice would *we* give *us*? If I could visit the college-aged me, I'd tell myself not to cry for literally an entire year over a man I'd dated a mere six weeks. I'd also ask myself to go easy on those Long Island Iced Teas. I'd stop myself from skipping morning lectures (I mean, hey it was costing a fortune) and I'd most definitely warn against drunken karaoke.

Fast forward to a meeting with 20-something me. I'd tell me that it didn't all have to mean so bloody much. That every breakup or lost temp job or car repair bill wasn't the end of the world. I'd say, "You won't even remember some of these names and dates and places. They are just fragments of an unfolding story, most of which will get deleted in the re-writes. They will not make the final cut." I'd also advise myself to not let my gas tank run on empty … or even below the line on occasion.

But, alas, there is no "Cecily from the future" option. There was and is only the present me, and I have to worm my way through my choices, just like everyone else. That said, I have asked my friends and colleagues to offer some insight based on their life lessons. Some of these they would prefer the opposite gender not to know, and some are merely suggestions based on suffering. But all are bits of wisdom that emerged after years of reflection and repeated patterns.

Think of this next chapter as the "you from the future" coming back to present day to give you a little heads up. It would have been nice, for example, if "future me" had let me in on the fact that spiking my hair just like '80s pop stars wouldn't work if my hair was curly. Thanks future me; thanks for nothing.

# CHAPTER 9

# From the Vault

Let's start with one of my cardinal rules:

## "FRIENDS WITH BENEFITS" SIMPLY DOES NOT WORK

I know there are a lot of folks out there who will disagree with this, mainly out of their own desire for it to not be true. But if I could take 20-something me into a room and yell the above sentence 100 times, I'd do it. This rule is one for women especially to hear (although I'm sure many men get hurt by it too) and although admitting it might not make me popular, I'm telling you, it's true.

As usual, let me start with a personal tale. I was dear friends with a boy we'll call Larry for years. We were in fact best friends…you know the kind who talk on the phone five times a day and have a thousand inside jokes. I adored Larry and always had just a little crush on him, but it was minor compared to my appreciation of his friendship.

One day at a friend's wedding (while trying to make an ex jealous, of course) I got just a tad bit drunk and insisted that Larry, who'd been my friend-date, slow dance with me. He did, it was awkward, and life went on as usual. But when we got to the car, the alcohol had infiltrated my grey matter and next thing I knew, I was snogging him. Larry, mind you, did not resist. We made out for hours. And then years went by. Although we laughed about it, nothing happened again.

Until my birthday three years later. Once again, I was single, and once again, I drank too much. Larry had helped me bring my birthday gifts up from the car and then next thing I knew, I was jumping him. This time it led into the bedroom, where our friendship was officially elevated (or demoted, whichever way you choose to look at it) into the gray zone.

For an entire year, Larry and I had a secret friends-with-benefits affair. He consistently told me he couldn't foresee a real relationship between us and he even refused to tell his other friends, which really hurt. But on and on we went, going through the motions of a love affair, without the love on his part. But (and does *this* sound familiar?) I was *sure* I could change his mind. I was positive that just one more night was all it would take to convince him that we belonged together. I'd wear sexy underwear, put on romantic music, all the stuff you're supposed to do to set a mood and he'd show up for it! But once again, I had gravely confused sex with love and friendship with romance. And by taking part in it, Larry was an accomplice.

## ONE PERSON WILL ALWAYS WANT MORE THAN THE OTHER

Make sure you fully appreciate that reality, because the one person just might be you. Okay, yes, you might be able to have one drunken night with a friend with minimal awkwardness. (Larry and I were, after all, able to do that the first time.) But if you consistently sleep with someone for any length of time, you are bound to develop feelings that go beyond friendship.

Women have a tougher time compartmentalizing our emotions, and thus are more likely to be the ones hurt in the end. And it's not that men knowingly disregard our feelings; they just assume that because *they're* able to separate sex from emotion, we can too. Of course, sometimes the guy is the one who develops feelings, but it doesn't really matter which gender ends up hurt. What matters is that the imbalance will likely not get resolved until the sex ends, and when that happens the friendship usually ends along with it.

People usually tell you how they feel and you must *listen*, even if it isn't what you want to hear. If a guy says, "I don't want to be your boyfriend" then guess what? He probably doesn't want to be your boyfriend. Just because you really, really *want* him to be (and he has sex with you on a regular or semi-regular basis) doesn't make it so. Believe me, Larry didn't mince words. We

can talk all day about how he should have made his actions match his declarations, but shouldn't I have known better? I made my educated, if stupid, choices, and I had to suffer (and suffer and suffer) the consequences.

And now here's a word of advice I would like to give to the "Larrys" out there: please don't string people along, especially not your friends. Yes, they can make their own decisions, but somewhere deep inside you are aware that morally you shouldn't be having both sex and a friendship with a person knowing there will never be a relationship. The "benefits" part really becomes overshadowed by all of the hurt and confusion it will most likely lead to.

And for the "me's" out there: What the hell are you thinking? Ask yourself just what is the line between a friendship and a romantic relationship. You might find that it doesn't really amount to formal "dates," but instead comes down to respect and expectations. If someone is claiming you're "just friends" but then having sex with you, really he's saying, "I like you okay, but what I really like is getting laid." Is that good enough for you? You most likely don't have to dig too deep for that answer. If he's *really* your friend, he'll understand when you say no. And to be honest, if he's really your friend he might say no to you when you're drunk, too.

## KEEP AN AIR OF MYSTERY

A buddy of mine insists that men and women get too comfy in relationships and forget how to seduce one another. We get so wrapped up in the boyfriend-girlfriend world that we forget how to be lovers. Not that there's anything wrong with good old-fashioned intimacy, and undoubtedly the best relationships have friendship at the core. But you don't have to trim your toenails in front of your companion or go to the bathroom while he brushes his teeth.

Many will disagree with this sentiment and claim that true intimate connection evolves from the ability to let your walls down. And while that is true to an extent, remember you're still lovers and it's a good idea to keep an element of surprise. Sure, be yourself, be comfortable, but ease up on stuff like, I don't know … burping the alphabet? Might be *kind* of funny the first few times, but is it really sexy? No.

I have to admit I might take this too far the other way. I think to this day I've never allowed a boyfriend to see my ass with the lights on (and if they

have, it's been by accident). Yeah I have ass issues and still tend to either back out of the bedroom after sex or grab whatever's nearby (e.g. his boxers) and cover myself up. However, this doesn't actually help ensure mystery, it only accentuates my insecurities, which also isn't very sexy.

There is an exception to this rule: for those out there who have a newborn and/or a job that keeps you working 50- to 60-hour weeks, you might not always have the time or energy to be fully shaved, clipped and mysterious. You absolutely, no-bones-about-it get a pass, whether you're a woman or man.

But for the rest of us who *do* have the time, try to invest in some sexy underwear or boxers now and again. It doesn't have to be something new every day or even every week, but make an attempt to wear something other than your stretched-out cotton underwear your mother gave you, or your paint-stained, threadbare T-shirt✱.

> ✱Note: I've spent many nights on the couch with boyfriends while wearing old Hall and Oates T-shirts and facial masks. I'm a complete hypocrite. There. I feel better having said that.

## BE THE PERSON YOU OBSESS OVER

I believe it was Gloria Steinem who once said: "Some of us are becoming the men we wanted to marry." I have always loved this quote, which I take to mean that instead of putting all our effort into bagging a great man, we ought to find that greatness in *ourselves*.

Now before I get into all this, I have a confession. The first time I heard this idea wasn't from Steinem, but rather from *Tiger Beat* magazine. I think it's clear by now that I was obsessed with Duran Duran, and Simon LeBon in particular. This lust/infatuation technically continues to this day, but back in the '80s it was especially intense. It became a compulsion to buy every poster, every b-record import, every magazine that featured Simon and the gang. I knew his favorite food, color, pastimes, his kissing style, dogs' names and favorite lipstick color. (*What?* It was the *'80s!*) Nothing else really mattered. I just wanted to know Simon LeBon and I wanted him to love me.

It had never occurred to me that instead of adoring *him*, I could become the kind of woman *he'd* adore. Essentially the rule is this: work on becoming fabulous and you'll attract fabulous people. Thankfully, the writers at *Tiger Beat* magazine had the foresight (or perhaps the moral obligation) to point out to us 13-year-olds that we needed to chill out. But the thing is, many of us still haven't really chilled. We're consumed with the notion that we must find a man (or if you're a guy, a woman) who will make us complete. We forget that we really have to do that for ourselves if we want to bring any kind of balance to a relationship.

I do wish I'd read that *Tiger Beat* article before I hurled my 85-pound body (I was 13!) onto the stage at a Howard Jones concert. (Howard was my back-up love when MTV took occasional breaks from playing Duran Duran videos.) There he stood, his spiky hair and weird accordion/keyboard combo in full swing, about to sing "What is Love" when my crazy seventh-grade ass made it past security and onto his feet. He just kind of gently shook his foot, like I was a little fly landing on his shoelace. What did I *think* he was gonna do? Tell the band to stop playing so he could further explore our relationship? Say: "Who *is* this awkward pre-teen groveling at my toes? Cecily, you say? Well hold the phone everybody. We're gonna have to reschedule this concert because I finally have found out what love is."

I was so dorky and small that security lifted me off the stage and put me back into my seat. I wasn't even enough of a threat to throw out of the show! But I still have hope that somewhere Howard remembers our magical night together. Wait, what was the topic again? Oh yeah, so next time you're ruminating over some musician, say because he plays the accordion/keyboard awesomely, instead find an instrument *you* play well. Let him obsess a little over you. I use this as an example and don't mean to say you should simply copy the talents of those with whom you're infatuated. It merely means you should find out who the hell you are and make it known what you have to offer. And if it's just being kind or funny or having the ability to hurl yourself past security … well, that's okay too.

## DON'T CONFUSE A RENDEZVOUS WITH A RELATIONSHIP

Okay now it's time to *really* let my crazy out. I can't believe I'm going to share the following story, but for the purpose of full disclosure I feel it's important everything's on the table. Oh dear. I really hope mental health officials can't find me after this.

So there I am on my first trip to London, a town I'd dreamt of going to my entire life. I meet a boy named Simon (not LeBon) who knows I'm an American anglophile who will melt from every little English trick in the book. He poshes up his accent and starts doing the Hugh Grant eye-flutter/stutter combo. I know it's contrived and put on and yet I fall for it because I'm in the mood to fall.

After a good number of unusually strong drinks (is the alcohol proof higher in the U.K.?) and after Simon whispers a few Shakespearian sonnets in my ear (really!) I agree to make out with him on the roof of the youth hostel. It's ridiculously romantic and British and Dickensian, without all the orphans and poverty and chimney sweeps, of course.

Simon's a wonderful kisser and extremely charming and it's exactly the kind of night I had in mind when I booked the trip. Because I'd made it abundantly clear that I had no intention of sleeping with him, the night comes to an end and Simon walks me from the roof to my dingy room and bids me a lovely farewell.

That's that, right? No, of course not. Because I'm *insane*. Now Simon and I hadn't traded last names, but he *had* disclosed that he had appeared in a bit part on some British TV detective show. Oh, did I mention Simon is an actor? The show is called *Inspector Morse* and is apparently quite popular among the Brits. So anyway, he kisses me good night and wishes me a great life back in "The States," blah, blah, blah.

A few months go by and (wow, I can't believe I'm telling this story) I'm back in California. I decide I'd like to *find* Simon, but I only have his first name and the knowledge that he had two lines on a TV show. I look him up on IMDb (a database for performers in TV and film) and it turns out that "Simon" is a very popular name in Great Britain. There are tons of them and I can't figure out which one he is.

Do I then decide it's not meant to be, get back to work and get on with my life? Nope. I contact the BBC. I was working for a famous actor's production company at the time so I was *technically* not lying when I said, "Hi, I work for a Los Angeles-based production company and am trying to locate an actor on *Inspector Morse*. His name is Simon and I know he filmed the show around this time last summer."

Since they were English, they were incredibly polite. "Ms. Knobler, we'd be more than delighted to help you on your quest. In fact, it will be quite fun." After only a week's time, I received another email from the BBC that read something like, "We are so pleased to tell you we have located the actor in question! His name is Simon (last name) and his contact info is as follows, (contact info). We do hope this has been of help to you and your production company and should we be of any more assistance, we'd be more than thrilled."

Well, *now* my crazy was wasting *everyone's* time. But I'd come this far and so I did what any hot-blooded, slightly (ha!) obsessive woman would do. I wrote a letter to Simon's agent and asked that they please pass on this note: "Had a great time with you in London and I think we should keep in touch. Here's my information, etc, etc." And I mailed it.

I never heard back from Simon (or his agent, for that matter). I did learn from this, though, that some moments should stay frozen on the rooftops of youth hostels and not be brought back to our home countries. This realization, however, did not stop me from recently finding him on Facebook. You'll be pleased to know I have refrained from contacting him … for now.

## UN-TAG!

All right, you Facebook users. Here's a wise pearl you probably won't get from a grandparent, so listen up. If you *are* lucky enough to be in a relationship but go out on the town with friends sans your companion, beware of that digital camera. Because once you've had some cocktails and that little point-and-click Canon starts flashing, you might forget that we live in a very public age. In my 20s if I found myself, say, draped over the lap of an open mic comedian while wearing, say, a latex full-body suit, there wouldn't have been much evidence. Now, there's very little one can do to *hide* the proof, thanks in part to Facebook, which allows your "friends" to tag your name in photos. Learn this word and say it with me: *Un-tag.* Pictures get posted of you doing tequila shooters at some place called "Crazies"? *Un-tag.* Some shots of you drunkenly humping a statute of Abraham Lincoln somehow appear online? *Un-tag.* You make an adult film with Paris Hilton and still photos get posted on the Facebook feed? That's right, *Un-tag.* Trust me on this one. And while we're on the topic, I don't need anyone else tagging my photos from when I was in the high-school mime troupe. *Un-tag, Un-tag, Un-tag.*

## FROM THE "MOM" VAULT

At some point in our lives, many of our mothers have imparted nuggets of wisdom to us. If we're lucky, that wisdom is feisty and relevant. In the case of my own mom, I'll say at least she got the feisty part down. Here are a few pieces of advice she has selflessly given to me over the years and I will now share them with you. You're welcome, in advance.

## BUYING THE COW

You've probably heard that old saying: "No one's gonna buy the cow if he gets the milk for free." This basically implies that men won't make "honest women" out of their companions (i.e., marry them) if these women give up sex before getting marriage in return. Here's what *my* mom actually said to me. "Cecily, no one's gonna take the cow to dinner if the cow keeps giving him blowjobs."

Gross. "*First* of all," I told her, "we no longer need the cow in the scenario. Second, that is disgusting and third … that's the *opposite* of true. That's exactly when a guy's gonna take you to dinner!"

We agreed to disagree.

## HALF A VALIUM A DAY KEEPS THE DOCTOR VERY BUSY

Somewhere along the way, my mom decided that if a woman is not enjoying being with a particular man on a date, then instead of ending the date and perhaps not accepting another, she should just take half a Valium and *make* herself like the man. So if, for example, my date is going on and on about how he loves Michael Bay movies and he grows weed in his basement with the hopes to fund his own directing career (yes this is a real person) I should pop half a muscle relaxant and simply pretend the boy had said "P.T. Anderson" instead of "Michael Bay." (Incidentally, the weed part didn't bother me so much.)

Sadly, this tactic is a failure and I strongly urge against it. And for the record, tequila shots work way better than Valium, anyway.

## SHUFFLEBOARD, ANYONE?

This one might be my favorite. My mom took me aside on my 16th birthday and said the following: "Don't ever break up with a man on vacation, especially a vacation that involves a ten-day cruise." It seems she made this mistake and according to her it led to some uncomfortable moments at the breakfast buffet. Not to mention, it must have been *really* awkward to bring a new suitor back to their shared cabin.

Now *that's* sage advice.

## FROM THE EXTRA-FUN HIDDEN VAULT

And now some insight in some naughtier areas. Here goes:

## ROLE PLAYING SHOULDN'T BE LITERAL

If you choose to have a little role-playing fun with your partner, try not to take it too seriously. Remember you are just playing and the objective is to get each other turned on, not win an Emmy. (Although wouldn't that be nice?)

I learned this the hard way, as I have a tendency to need a little bit of truth in my fantasies. I can't just assume the role of the sexy teacher or sexy nurse in my role-playing; there has to be more of a purpose. So, for example, a boy-friend asked that we play naughty nurse/sexy patient. I said to him, "Okay Mr. Walters, it's time for your sponge bath. Are you ready for your sponge bath?"

He of course replied, "Yes," nodding his head.

"Well why don't you take off your clothes then?"

He took off his clothes.

"Ok, here we go. Oh wait, it says here you're HMO isn't paid in full. I'm sorry, Mr. Walters, you're a bad, bad man and I can't help you."

That put an end to *that*. It happened another time when the same boy-friend suggested we play hottie/construction worker. I put on my cute little plaid skirt and he whistled at me from across the room. "Hey sexy Mamma," he said, "Let me see that ass."

I walked over to him and said, "Oh, so *you're* my baby daddy?! I've been looking for you for ages! I have a petition for child support." Once again, this failed to turn him on.

My point it is that if you do decide to role-play, you don't have to have a whole script written out. Just have fun with your characters and try not to mention real-life downers like "health insurance" and "divorce court." For some reason, it doesn't seem to get people in the mood.

## BE YOUR OWN KEY MASTER

A female friend was kind enough to share this pearl of wisdom: if you're gonna use handcuffs in bed, know where the key is. Seems simple enough and yet I've heard many stories where couples have gotten excited by the idea of what I call "pedestrian bondage." This means they want to explore a little S&M, but want to keep it safe. These are the folks who think handcuffs are the kinkiest item one can bring into the bedroom. (Aren't they just adorable?!)

So they try it, but in all their excitement, they toss the key and then spend three anxious hours trying to find it when they should really be enjoying their little game of cops and robbers. Also, if you don't care too much about authenticity, I recommend trying the fuzzy handcuffs, as they are far more comfortable than the real deal.

> "God breaks the heart again and again and again,
> until it stays open."
>
> — Hazrat Inayat Khan

While I was writing this book, I happened to get a Facebook message from J.J. Nesbitt. You might recall him from the first chapter as the guy who ran screaming to the teacher when I tried to kiss him during four square. He was polite and inquisitive as to what I'd been doing all these years and after a few exchanged emails, we started a game of online Scrabble.

I finally got up the nerve to ask him if he remembered the day I tried to kiss him and he subsequently called me a "psycho mamma." He wrote something back like "LOL [which was annoying] I don't remember that! Are you sure that was me? I'd never have refused a kiss from *you*."

But we all know he *did* refuse the kiss and told me I was crazy for even wanting one. To be fair, we were only 10 years old and somehow I was able to continue muddling through my life. But had I known he would hit on me (at least in the virtual world) years later, I probably wouldn't have sweated it so much.

So he had thought I was crazy. To *him* (and I'd assume many boys his age) the idea of trying to press your lips up to anything besides a BLT *is* crazy. And I thought *he* was nuts for not getting it. The word "crazy" only became harder to hear later in life when I inferred it to mean there was something wrong with me.

I've spent years trying to figure out why it crushes me so much to hear negativity from the opposite sex. If a female friend is upset with me, sure I'm irritated, but I have a tendency to deflect it back onto *her*. I have an unfortunate ability to write off girlfriends with relative ease. Yet if a *guy* has words for me (particularly a boyfriend), I internalize everything and believe it to be true. Then I spend an inordinate amount of time trying to prove him wrong.

Lots of men I've spoken to have the same issue. If a male buddy calls them an asshole, they laugh and share a beer. But if it comes from a woman they might pretend not to care but on the inside will be saying, "Wait, *am* I an asshole?"

We get under each other's skin in a way that keeps many of us in constant doubt. Based on the number of stories I've heard of relationships gone wrong, I think it's fair to make this statement. And speaking of numbers of stories, now might be a good time to let you know that (thank goodness) there has been some overlap throughout this book. Sometimes the same guy has starred in two or more anecdotes; for example, the "friends with benefits" guy was also the religious zealot. Hmm, that makes you wonder, doesn't it?

# CHAPTER 10

# Is she crazy?
# Does he lie?
# Does it matter?

Perspective is a funny thing. It has everything to do with how we feel and how we perceive events, and it explains how two people can see a situation – and even abstract notions like love and indifference – completely differently. Differing perspectives are the culprit in so many misunderstandings and heartbreaks.

The key is this: if you know at your core who you are and you act from that core with the most integrity possible, it will be harder for external sources to make you doubt yourself. It doesn't mean you won't be hurt in relationships at times. You'll just hopefully have a better chance at bouncing back more quickly.

I have a friend who has more resilience after getting her heart broken than anyone I've ever known. Sure she has mourned the losses of boyfriends, but because she's so sure of who she is, she never doubts the eventual outcome. She never says to herself things like, "I was too controlling, that's why he left," or "Am I crazy?" or "Is it over because I'm too needy?"

This is not to say she never questions her part in the relationship's downfall. She just doesn't put all of the blame on her and instead has the ability to ask, for example, "Why does *he* have a problem with being needed?" She is able to remember her own wonderful qualities and say, "I'll miss him, but it really is his loss." She maintains a positive attitude and then instead of bringing baggage into the next relationship, she brings enlightenment.

I, on the other hand, have not been able to do this. Instead I internalize it all. Once, a guy broke up with me claiming I was too "depressed." I could have said to myself, "Who needs a fair-weather boyfriend anyway? I'm glad I dodged *that* bullet!" But instead I said, "What's wrong with me? Why *can't* I be in a great mood all the time?"

For the record, that guy dumped me for a certifiable moron. What made it worse was she was trying to pursue a career in stand-up comedy (he and I were both comics) and she literally told hack jokes about how people of different races drive differently. I mention all of this because A) the fact that she was a bad comedian made me feel better and B) I realized that if he wanted *her*, we'd never have worked. (Just FYI, they broke up when she started doing jokes about tampons. Like I said ... moron.)

## SO ... IS SHE CRAZY?

Let's take a look at some of the reasons guys might call women nuts (or psycho or crazy or any of the rest of those descriptive terms).

Another common term is "too emotional." What this term really means: *too* emotional, for some men, means showing *any* emotion at all. A woman might tear up at a Bud Light commercial (ahem) and a guy will say she's histrionic. Is it our "fault"? Is there really even such thing as "fault" in this situation? What does it matter?

If some of us cry more, so *what*? Women have a whole different makeup than men, which makes it easier both biochemically and socially to tap into their emotions. This doesn't make us any more crazy than a man is crazy for having a lower voice.

Does this mean we need to run around screaming and crying all the time? Of course not. As with any emotional reaction, whether sadness, delight, anger, jealousy or any other, there's a time and place for expression and subtlety is often appreciated. But are we "psycho" if we feel strongly about something? No. (An exception here is during a breakup. In that case, let's wear our "crazy" proudly.)

Perhaps the word "clingy" comes to mind when thinking of some women. I've heard boys use this word more than once when describing their girlfriends (and/or exes). Whereas some men have a tendency to want to keep their options open, women are more likely to go into lock-it-down mode, wherein they want the relationship defined more quickly than a guy might. This can lead to what men perceive as clinginess in women, when really they're simply insecure. While this might not be attractive to men, it certainly doesn't make us "crazy."

How 'bout that old word, "naggy?" I've noticed the "nag" word gets thrown around more times than the "L" word and it can pop out of a man's mouth at the slightest provocation. "Hey, would you mind *not* leaving your dirty sweaty socks on the dining room table?" or "Hey, did you remember to feed our baby while I was out of town for three days?" or "Yo, would it be possible to *not* have sex with the nanny while I'm sleeping?"

These kinds of questions might be met with "Nag, nag, nag … that's all you women do." Sometimes just asking a question seems to be met with the nag accusation. So when a woman, for example, says, "Hon, what time did you want to go out tonight?" and the man continues watching TV, saying nothing, she'll ask again, "Baby, did you hear me?" That right there could be perceived as nagging, when really she's just frustrated by his lack of response.

But there *are* times when women just need to drop it. Men don't want to be treated like they're children and sometimes, even when they're not being treated that way, they *perceive* themselves to be. If you ask a guy a question and he's in Douchey McGee mode, then very little good can come from repeating a question 10 times. Once he realizes he's being ridiculous he'll answer your question or mow the lawn or whatever it is he's committed to do.

And my advice for the guys is: Don't act like children and we won't treat you like them! In a grown-up relationship, both parties must treat the other with equal respect. This means even if you're annoyed by something (and yes, we all get annoyed) you have to at least be responsive. If this means saying something like, "I hear you. I'm just gonna watch this show and then I'll be

right there," then so be it. Unless it's a dire situation, that should be good enough. And think about the situation a little before screaming. Maybe *she's* not pissed because you won't mow the lawn; maybe she's pissed because she has to ask. Maybe *he's* not pissed because she's asking, but because he doesn't want to be told what to do. All this being said, when pressed, men admit they use the word "nag" to get what they want, because no woman wants to be seen as one. As soon as the guy brings out the "n" word, we shut up and he gets his way. And they say *we're* manipulative.

Yes we all have our extreme moments (and okay, maybe extreme years) and yes, to someone or a few someones out there, we might be considered a crazy ex. But we can also be so much more. To someone *else*, we're the one who got away, or we're the one worth fighting for. It all just depends on who's telling the story.

## IS HE A LIAR?

Just as it's dubious to deem all women crazy, it's probably a tad unfair to say all men lie. I mean, yes, some guys lie. In fact, nearly all *people* lie at some points in their lives. It might even be fair to say that some of us lie every day without even really thinking about it: "I love that dress," or "Your band sounded great."

Before we start pointing fingers at boys, I have to address the fact that women obviously lie in relationships too. (I mean, c'mon, right?) Aside from the more tragic crimes some of us commit, such as infidelity, how 'bout when a woman might tell a guy, "don't call" when she really means "*call!*" I think we went through some of this in the "Rules" section. We lie. We lie to each other and we lie, worst of all, to ourselves. But we're talking about the boys right now, so let's have a look:

Men are often purported to lie out of fear. Remember this is about perception, so if a man perceives that he might get a reaction he'd rather not deal with, he might fib to avoid it. Is fear the same thing as avoidance? In some cases, sure. And in some cases, it's even understandable.

But sometimes it's not understandable. Romantic relationships, whether they're emotional, sexual or both, lay our hearts bare and delicate. And when men (or anyone) lie about this or in a way that affects this, it's not okay – plain

and simple. So what about when they say they love you and then dump you? Are they lying or did they simply have a change of heart?

Sometimes I'm not sure *anyone* really knows. Feelings about love and lust and sex and jealousy all tend to get so mixed in with each other, it's hard to pick each emotion out. What love means to one person can't be exactly the same as what it means to another. So when, for example, a man says, "I meant it at the time," we're not even sure what *it* was.

## THE DEAL:

I'm gonna leave you with one more story in hopes that if nothing else, you'll feel better about your *own* choices in life. When I was 14, my junior high school (go Warriors!) had a talent show. Now I wasn't particularly popular, but I prided myself on being a kind of dark-haired Molly Ringwald type circa *Pretty in Pink*. (See how everything comes back to Blane?)

But the thing was, I didn't have any "Blanes" around me. Instead I had something like a hundred Duckies and that's way off-balance. Speaking of off-balance, a few months before the talent show, I wrote a poem in my journal about a guy I barely knew named Todd Keith. The poem went like this, "The bloody tears of a clown slide down my smile when you aren't in algebra class. Let us say goodbye to the silver worms of reality and welcome our reward … death." What this had to do with my interest in him, I'll never know, but I guess this helps exemplify that we all express love differently. As you can no doubt see, I was a very well-adjusted middle-schooler.

So, back to the talent show. I knew I'd never have the nerve to read that poem to Todd (until now) but still I had to do something drastic. So in front of 900 students I sang Depeche Mode's "Somebody," and in my mind, I was singing directly to him. I'm pretty sure he wasn't even there that day, but this didn't stop me from putting on an angora sweater (inspired by Howard Jones) changing all the "she's" in the song to "he's" and singing my heart out.

Some people might think this was a crazy move on my part. And I guess my point to all this is: so what if it was? I survived, Todd survived and Depeche Mode went on to make many more records. (Granted, I did feel it was best to leave that school system shortly after, even though the students were far kinder about the song than they needed to be.)

I guess if I could make just one deal with everyone it would be that we accept the fact that we all have different points of view. We would realize that, man or woman, we're gonna bring our own pile of baggage. And if we're lucky, some of those heavy bags will get lost along the way.

We can only hope for each other and ourselves that as we evolve, we get better and better with each friendship or relationship we encounter. And if there's any kind of positive spin I could put on my *own* personal crazy bag, it would be that at least I didn't sing a ballad by Air Supply.

# AcKnowLedgments

Much love and gratitude to my friends who have had to endure my heart-breaks and serotonin deficiency throughout the years, particularly Sheryl W., Debbie, Robyn L., Jen, Stef W., Laura S., Andy B., Greg W., Greg S., Lucy R., Ilyse M., Dave M. and the Family Dinner/Brass Monkey gang; my dear love Jeff Ghere; Wendy Morley and Bob Kennedy for making  this so much fun; Cal Slayton for his fabulous art work; my family for their love, humor and support, especially my brother Jeffrey, Claude, my wonderful mom, who taught me that indeed a "little lipstick wouldn't kill me" and my dad, for being such a great man that the bar has been set ridiculously high.